"G.F. Watkins is a doer, not a talker, he's a man who does not practice what he preaches, but preaches what he practices."

-Dr. Edwin Louis Cole

"G.F. Watkins is a coach in every sense of the word. I love playing on his team."

-Joe White

"Pastor Wakins is not only a man with a great vision but a man willing to do whatever it takes to see his vision come alive."

-Pastor Bill Wilson

"I have known Pastor G.F. Watkins for over ten years. I have witnessed his character, his purity, and his love for God. The "Alpha Male" is not a temperament or personality of some men but exposes deep, inner truths about what it really means to be "male." It is not a domineering or narcissistic mentality but rather a leadership by serving mentality. Truly, the strongest men are the deepest lovers of their wives. May the Lord use this tool to help a generation of men understand themselves and rise to lead our nation back to greatness!"

-Larry Stockstill
Author, Pastor of Bethany Church,
Baton Rogue, LA for 28 years.

Pastor GF has identified exactly what the issue is today with our economy, our nation and the church. It is the man. He clearly states what is required to become a man of God and challenges men to do it. Pastor Watkins is a pillar and role model for walking exactly what he is talking in the book, *"Alpha Male."*

-Darrel Billups, Th.D.
NCMM, Executive Director
National Coalition of Ministries to Men

THE ALPHA MALE

AND THE WOMEN WHO GET THEM

G. F. WATKINS

www.xulonpress.com

DEDICATION

I dedicate this book to every military soldier our nation has produced, who returned home to find a people oblivious to their sacrifice and families that couldn't understand them and to every coach that attended every practice with his athletes and still suffered persecution on Friday night from people who sit in the stands.

I dedicate this book to every pastor who laid down his life for his sheep, giving up time with his family, only to have them desert him or be disloyal.

I dedicate this book to every father who brought home a paycheck each week to give his wife and children a nice home, meals, clothes, and education, only to be rewarded with disrespect because he wasn't an Oscar winning movie star or Bill Gates, and because he refused to give in to social pressures knowing it would corrupt his children. They are the Alpha Males that quietly make our world a better place. I hope someone will listen.

In the movie, **"A Few Good Men,"** Jack Nicholson's character is definitely a secular Alpha Male. He is frustrated with the lack of knowledge exhibited in the courtroom about his life's calling. While I want to go on record as saying that I disagree with the character's actions concerning having a Marine beaten to death, if we listen real close we can hear the thoughts of a sacrificial man:

> Jessup: You can't *handle* the truth! Son, we live in a world that has walls, *and those walls have to be guarded by men with guns. Who's gonna do it? You? You, Lieutenant Weinberg? I have a greater responsibility than you can possibly fathom. You weep for Santiago and you curse the Marines. You have that luxury. You have the luxury of not knowing what I know, that Santiago's death, while tragic, probably saved lives. And my existence, while grotesque and incomprehensible to you, saves lives! You don't want the truth, because deep down in places you don't talk about at parties, you want me on that wall. You need me on that wall. We use words like "honor, code, and loyalty." We use these words as the backbone of a life spent defending something. You use them as a punchline. I have neither the time nor the inclination to explain myself to a man who rises and sleeps under the blanket of the very freedom that I provide, and then questions the manner in which I provide it! I would rather you just said "thank you," and went on your way. Otherwise, I suggest you pick up a weapon, and stand a post. Either way, I don't give a damn what you think you are entitled to!*

If I was attempting to be politically correct or religiously astute, I would leave this excerpt from this movie out. I'm not. I believe we have neutered real men in an attempt to pacify society for far too long. It's time we begin to recognize what real good men look like.

I dedicate this book to real good men! We need you.

ACKNOWLEDGMENTS

I want to acknowledge my father, Gayle Watkins Jr., Dr. Edwin Louis Cole, Pastor Larry Stockstill, and Pastor Walter Hallam for helping me to grow up. Each one of them has added to my life and helped me to appreciate an Alpha Male's contribution to this life and the one to come.

I'd also like to acknowledge the members and staff of Power House Church in Katy, Texas and Jordan Ranch for supporting this ministry as well as my family for the past twenty years. You are excellent!

Finally, I'd like to thank my wife, Rose for supporting our ministry to God's people for over twenty-five years. I know firsthand how difficult it is to live with an Alpha, we are just now figuring it out! Thanks for fighting for our marriage through it all. I've learned the most right here.

My dad, Gayle Watkins, my hero. The older I get, the wiser he seems!

TABLE OF CONTENTS

Foreword xv

Preface: The Alpha Male...*and the women*
that get them xix

Chapter 1:   What Is an Alpha Male? 27

Chapter 2:   Endangered Species 39

Chapter 3:   Winning 51

Chapter 4:   What Every Alpha Male Needs to Know
About Women 61

Chapter 5:   Oxygen 77

Chapter 6:   Desperado. 91

Chapter 7:   Honor 101

Chapter 8:   Alpha and Omega 121

Chapter 9:   Fruit. 131

Chapter 10: Truths I Shared With My Sons 159

Chapter 11: Sacrifice Goes with the Territory 175

Conclusion: Get Ready for War 187

Postscript. 193

FOREWORD
BY LT. GENERAL WILLIAM G. "JERRY" BOYKIN (RET.)

The Alpha Male is a concept that we generally reserve for the animal kingdom. This timely and powerful book you are holding makes the case that men are designed and intended to be Alpha Males, and Pastor G.F. Watkins poignantly illustrates how men are invited to embrace the immense but rewarding responsibilities of this calling.

I spent thirty-six years in the U.S. Army, serving most of my career in Special Operations, Rangers, Delta Force, and Special Forces. In that time, I served with some real men, true Alpha Males, who embodied the characteristics outlined in this book. An "alpha male" is tough, decisive, and courageous, a man with strong resolve and an empathetic heart. They are men who know that these characteristics define every role they take on in life, roles as husbands, fathers, and leaders at all levels.

In the animal kingdom, the Alpha Male is the pack unifier, the single, greatest reason that packs survive, especially in difficult times. Men who take on the Alpha Male role in the family or community have the same responsibility, to unite their pack by creating an atmosphere of harmony, and reducing conflicts that may arise within their sphere.

God is clear in His word that men have a responsibility to be leaders in the home, the community, the church, and on the job. Men who fail to realize that God has called them to lead are generally failures in life. It is certain that some men are more adept at leading than others, but failing to step up to opportunities of leadership each day and embracing the responsibilities that God places on the heart are inexcusable failures for a Christian man.

American society is suffering from an epidemic of fatherless homes. Children growing up in homes without fathers are statistically less likely to succeed in life than those raised in a two-parent home consisting of a mother and father. Rather than seeing themselves as Alpha Males with responsibilities for leadership in the home, too many men are seeing themselves as sperm donors with no responsibilities for rearing the offspring. Our nation suffers greatly from this self-perpetuating pattern among men. Men are to teach the next generation to be men, or better stated, to bring up the next generation of Alpha Males. When there is no Alpha Male in the home, how are these traits to be taught to the next generation?

God's directive in 1 Peter 3:1 to women which says, "Wives, likewise, be submissive to your own husbands...", places a tremendous burden on the man. A man who has not yet achieved The Alpha Male status in life is far more likely to take that directive as an opportunity to ignore his wife's needs and to focus solely on having his own needs met. The true Alpha Male recognizes the responsibility that comes with this and recognizes the imperative to defend the wife with his life. In other words, he becomes her protector. Furthermore, he accepts his role as a provider for the needs of the family that his wife has borne him. Money is not all that he provides for the wife and family. The Alpha Male father and husband provides identity and direction.

The Alpha Male also provides spiritual direction and context for the family. He is expected to know the word of God and to be able to apply its principles in his own life and to set an example for his children and wife of what a godly man is. World events must be explained from a biblical world view. The Alpha Male must be capable of explaining to children what "turn the other cheek" means and how it is applied in an increasingly dangerous world where terrorists cheer the murder of Christians in horrible and inhumane acts of brutality. The Alpha Male understands the idea of spiritual warfare and strives to prepare his family and those around him for battle. He sets the example for being willing to step into battle for a transcendent cause, a cause worth fighting and sacrificing for. His ability to inspire others to understand and accept their calling in service to the Lord is a leadership trait that benefits everyone around him.

Pastor Watkins has captured the essence of this concept of the Alpha Male because he is an Alpha Male himself. A tough athlete and a godly man, G.F. Watkins has lived his life as a husband, father, pastor, coach, and community leader in an admirable manner. What he writes about in his book reflects his own experience as well as the wisdom passed on to him from some incredible mentors, including his own role model, his father. This book could not be more timely and valuable. It will help breed a new generation of Alpha Males.

William G. "Jerry" Boykin *was the United States Deputy Undersecretary of Defense for Intelligence under President George W. Bush from 2002 to 2007 and is a conservative Christian political activist. During his thirty-six-year career in the military, he spent thirteen years in the Delta Force, including two years as its commander, and was involved in numerous high-profile missions, including the 1980 Iran hostage rescue attempt, the 1992 hunt for Pablo Escobar in Colombia, and the Black Hawk Down incident in Mogadishu, Somalia. He is an author and teaches at Hampden-Sydney College, Virginia. He is currently executive vice president at the Family Research Council.*

PREFACE

Her mightiest warriors no longer fight.
They stay in their barracks, their courage gone.
They have become like women.
The invaders have burned the houses
and broken down the city gates.
(Jeremiah 51:30 NLT)

Our men are lost. The pendulum has swung way to the left. Our nation and our world need men of character, integrity, single-mindedness, COURAGE and maturity to stand up and begin to reverse the curse of apathy, weak-mindedness, complacency, and cowardice that has gripped this once proud and powerful nation. To reverse the curse, it will take many working together in biblical unity. The experience is available now. The tools are available now. The team is available now. The willing heart to offer the help is available now.

The Alpha Male Statement of Belief

Strong churches exist because the men in them are strong in their faith and their courage. When we use the term church, keep in mind the first churches were called the *ecclesia* or the set apart ones. They were set part because of their sacrificial hearts. These were people who understood the fact that if they joined this set apart group, they would be killed for a cause bigger than themselves. The first church was a group of ultimate warriors. The eternal prize is still the ultimate cause for a man to lay down his life.

The following thoughts are my effort to expose why I feel it is time to plant truths in the local church that will strengthen the men and thereby strengthen the church.

- The majority of churches worldwide are composed of a ratio of 80 percent female members and 20 percent male members. The Bible is written to men and initially intended to be taught to men in a congregational setting. The men, as heads of their homes, would then be responsible for taking this information back and leading their homes in the implementation of these truths.
- You can have spirituality (worship, praise, atmosphere, righteousness, etc.) with women, but it takes godly, courageous men to bring strength, action, warfare, discipline, direction, leadership, single-mindedness, and decisiveness to the Church.
- The above-mentioned percentages show us a matriarchal or mother led country, family, and church which depletes the attributes of a male or father figure. For example, a male is more prone to discipline with a physical force like a spanking or push-ups, while a female is more prone to discipline with her words. A current example of this can be seen in two presidents. President George W. Bush

was raised with a father in his home so when America was under attack on 9/11, he responded decisively and almost immediately with military force. President Obama was raised in a matriarchal environment therefore he tries diplomatic or verbal means to rectify threatening situations. When we enter most churches we see young urban metro sexual males with a liberal political view, who wear skinny jeans, grooms his eyebrows, colors his hair with streaks of yellow, does his nails, and is interested in the latest and greatest TV fads. Immature males are adapting to the culture of a feminine church and have little heart for sacrifice.

- Evangelizing the man is actually the pattern of the Bible. Jesus picked twelve men disciples to change the world. God came in the form of a man, Jesus, to illustrate roles of leadership and sacrifice from a man's perspective.

- When a child is the first person saved in a family there is a **3 percent** chance the rest of his family will be saved. When the mother is the first to be saved, the percentage increases to **13 percent.** When the **man/father** is first to be saved, the percentage increases to **95 percent**. The man is the ultimate influencer even though he is usually more difficult to win over.

- A man hears a different tune than a woman. He has a different language that he responds to. To minister to men effectively, we need to know their language, learn what attracts them, discover what challenges them to action, and discern what motivates their hearts. A man needs a different message to keep his **sacrificial** leadership rightly focused. Men are designed to lay down their lives, but a matriarchal message tells them they need to preserve it. A real man understands that some things are more important than life itself.

For the husband is head of the wife, as also Christ is head of the church; and He is the Savior of the body. Husbands, love your wives, just as Christ also loved the church and gave Himself for her. (Ephesians 5:23, 25 NKJV)

- Affirmation comes from a father (man) to a son (man). A woman cannot affirm a man. We have a 40 percent divorce rate in our country. This translates to most young men being raised by single mothers. The model of femininity begins in our homes and then bleeds over into our churches which are a picture of our society. The church with the message of manhood and Christ-likeness is poised as never before to be the catalyst that reverses the curse in our men and then our society.

So what do we actually need to do that begins this process in our churches?

1. Teach pastors how to speak a man's language and disciple men. Use the Ed Cole curriculum with books like "Maximized Manhood," "Courage," "Sexual Integrity,"

> "Being a male is a matter of birth, being a man is a matter of choice."—Ed Cole

"Communication, Sex, and Money," "Real Man," etc. in a classroom setting as well as in a self-paced study group until these truths become infused in the men of the church.

2. Hold a commissioning ceremony annually which recognizes the accomplishments of the men in front of the church and their families. The men must know their role so they can reach their goal. (We can help you with this process.)

3. Help the pastor identify solid elders (pastor gifts) and deacons (task gifts). Once identified, they should help to establish the pastor as the leader in the eyes of the church family. This team should biblically teach honor towards their leader, who acts in many ways as the father of the church family. Finally, help the pastor to understand the purpose and power that his inner core of men possess so that he can use them efficiently.

> **OUR goal is to be godly husbands, fathers, sons, employees, business owners, politicians, and community leaders.**

What I see most in men around the world is that they feel more comfortable preaching to women. This is not God's best. What I see and hear is men opening up a storefront church and women running to it so they can facilitate their inner **"help mate."** Here is the problem, though. The ladies go home and proceed to tell their husbands what their new "man" just told them God said for them to begin to do. Most men stay on the golf course on Sundays or in front of the TV because they do not see the message of the preacher as relevant to their manhood. When the woman returns home to tell her man what

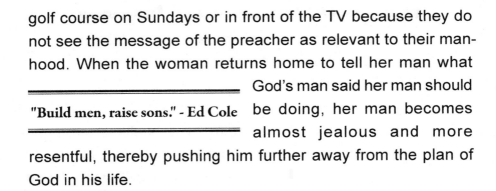

"Build men, raise sons." - Ed Cole

God's man said her man should be doing, her man becomes almost jealous and more resentful, thereby pushing him further away from the plan of God in his life.

Why Isn't the Church Influencing the World?

In our home city of Houston Texas, we have the largest attended church in the USA in Lakewood and Second Baptist is not far behind with 40,000 attendees on a Sunday morning. Yet we do not demonstrate the influence that it takes to vote out a homosexual mayor. To me the strength of our church should be demonstrated in our ability to influence our local community, not simply meet on Sunday morning to listen to a Bible story. Women will congregate in our churches; men will follow to get their check mark, make their mothers and wives happy, and keep the peace at home. But will they act on the truths preached each Sunday?

I heard an interesting message recently that captures this thought and I'd like to share it with you here. A man asked his teenage daughter to go to her room and clean it. She immediately went to the room with a pad and pen. She returned 30 minutes later having a full pad of notes taken. She informed her father that she had gone into her room and written down everything he had asked her to do. She presented him the pad with her notes on it. She felt she had finished what had been asked of her. Yet she had failed to clean her room.

Before you become upset at the girl, can we take a look at what most people consider a fulfilling church service on a Sunday morning? Aren't we guilty of a similar act when we are commanded, for example, to go forth and make disciples each week and we respond with a notepad full of sermon notes? It's our job to turn the truth we know into actions, isn't it? Men desire these types of challenges. They really desire a leader that measures their effectiveness just as they do on the job.

Another illustration of complacency came when I went to the dentist. The hygienist asked me if I flossed. Well like most people, I flossed the night before and that morning because I figured I would be asked that question. My answer was, yes, I floss, based on a limited definition of flossing.

She laughed and said, "Let me restate my question. Do you floss daily?" My answer was, "No. However, I do own dental floss." My point is that many of us consider ourselves flossers the way we consider ourselves Christians. We own floss, we go to church, we own a Bible, but we never quite get around to using it for the purpose it was and is intended for.

The entire earth is waiting, groaning, and travailing for men to be led by God's Holy Spirit to take a stand against the enemy that is out to destroy our families, our communities, and our nation. This is the Alpha Male that God designated to stand. God is, in essence, still screaming, **"Adam, where are you?"**

We are planting more churches today than ever before, yet crime is higher, divorce is higher, and abortion is higher than ever. To plant churches that will eventually become weak in their effectiveness cannot be our ultimate goal. We have the ability to plant confrontational, community changing houses of strength and light where the men are sacrificial and the women are covered and free to exercise their gifting alongside these men. We must be **intentional as well as strategic.**

This book is about what I have learned after ministering to men for over twenty-five years. I have taken what I have learned and done my best to communicate what strong men would like to say to the women, children, and others who surround them. They are good, hard-working men who desire the best in life for themselves and for their families. I pray this book helps you as a man to realize that there is a purpose for your personality. You are that you are not alone on this planet no matter how many sitcoms degrade your existence, you are the winner.

This book is also for women married to Alpha Males. If you can retain the wisdom from this book on how to facilitate your relationship with your Alpha Male father or husband, then this book is a success.

CHAPTER 1

WHAT IS AN ALPHA MALE?

They are cool. They are confident. They walk into a room and everybody stops and notices. When they speak, other guys listen. Guys want to hang out with them. Women want to go out with them. They are:

Alpha Males.

An Alpha Male has certain unmistakable characteristics. He is a natural leader. He is a pack builder. He leads, provides for, and protects his pack (his woman, buddies, teammates, and children).

The changing world presents a continuing opportunity for an Alpha Male. Where other guys see change as crisis, an Alpha Male is in his natural element. He continually observes cause and effect, and turns every opportunity to the advantage of his pack. He loves to win and is good at it.

> Often laid back until there is a need for action, an Alpha Male is fearless in a necessary fight. He is the best leader of men there is.

He is unconcerned with his image. He just goes about winning the game at hand, whatever it may be, and others follow.

They copy his style, speech, and look. An Alpha Male never copies anyone else. He is authentic.

Eight Giveaways You Are an Alpha Male

1. She never pays for dinner. An Alpha Male provides for his pack. If she tries to contribute to this, he calmly takes the check and says, "I will handle this." End of discussion.

2. An Alpha Male apologizes instantly. He has no hang ups. He simply says, "I was wrong. I apologize." Then he rectifies the problem if possible.

3. An Alpha Male is the leader. He does not suck up to anyone.

4. An Alpha Male never builds himself up by tearing others down. He never gossips about his boss, his buddies, or his girlfriend. An Alpha Male never betrays his pack.

5. An Alpha Male's natural element is change. Rapid change is simply an interesting challenge to him. He goes into a special kind of ice cold, almost detached state, quickly sums up the situation, does due diligence if time allows for it, and acts immediately and decisively based on prior experience if there is no time to spare.

6. An Alpha Male takes responsibility for his own actions. He never blames others.

7. An Alpha Male is not a liar. He shoots straight. He does not have to slither out of a mess he got himself into. He does what is right, and lets the chips fall where they may.

8. An Alpha Male takes on a real fight when it is necessary, and only if it is necessary. Alphas are not "scrappers."

He will not think twice about taking on someone bigger/stronger/ better-situated than he is if the matter being decided is serious. Due to his fierce drive, chances are good he will win.

A Christian example of an Alpha Male: Leonard Ravenhill

Great industrial concerns have in their employ men who are needed only when there is a breakdown somewhere. When something goes wrong with the machinery, these men spring into action to locate and remove the trouble and get the machinery rolling again. For these men, a smoothly operating system has no interest.

In the kingdom of God things are not too different. God has always had His specialists whose chief concern has been the moral breakdown and the decline in the spiritual health of the nation or the church. Such men were Elijah,

> They are specialists concerned with trouble and how to find and correct it.

Jeremiah, Malachi, and others of their kind who appeared at critical moments in history to reprove, rebuke, and exhort in the name of God and righteousness.

A thousand or ten thousand ordinary priests, pastors or teachers could labor quietly almost unnoticed while the spiritual life of Israel or the church was normal. Let the people of God go astray from the paths of truth, though, and immediately the specialist appeared almost out of nowhere. His instinct for trouble brought him on the scene at just the right time.

Such a man was likely to be drastic, radical, and possibly at times violent. The curious crowd that gathered to watch him work soon branded him as extreme, fanatical, and negative. In a sense they were right. He was single-minded, severe, and fearless because these were the qualities the circumstances demanded. He shocked some, frightened others, and alienated more than a few, but he knew who had called him and what he was sent to do.

To such men as this the church owes a debt too heavy to pay. The curious thing is that she seldom tries to pay him while he lives, but the next generation builds his sepulcher and writes his biography, as if instinctively and awkwardly to discharge an obligation the previous generation to a large extent ignored.

> **His ministry was geared to the emergency, and that fact marked him as different, a man set apart.**

Those who know Leonard Ravenhill will recognize him as the religious specialist, the man sent from God not to carry on the conventional work of the church, but to challenge the priests of Baal on their own mountain top, to shame the careless priest at the altar, to face the false prophet, and warn the people who are being led astray by him.

Such a man as this is **not an easy companion**. The professional evangelist who leaves the meeting as soon as it is over to go to the most expensive restaurant to feast and crack jokes with his retainers will find this man something of an embarrassment. He cannot turn off the burden of the Holy Ghost as one would turn off a faucet. He insists upon being a Christian all the time, everywhere. That marks him as different.

To Leonard Ravenhill, it is impossible to be neutral. His acquaintances are divided pretty neatly into two classes. They are those who love and admire him out of all proportion and those who hate him with perfect hatred.

Leonard Ravenhall is a great Christian example of a pioneer who tends to rub people wrong periodically because of the way he focuses and pursues truth. Dr. Ed Cole was this way as well. Jack King who served Dr. Cole as his point person for sixteen years told me one day the definition of a true prophet. He said, "Dr. Cole could see the end from the beginning and if something were to get into the way of the objective being reached, he would be quick to remove the obstacle even to the point where the average person might consider him to be gruff or rude. I believe he was simply focused."

In trying to make these men fit into our social norm, we actually neutralize their God given calling and potential to complete His will. Rather, we need to learn to help them be successful so that we all win.

Other Examples of Alpha Males

Douglas MacArthur: MacArthur had a long association with the Philippines including three separate tours of duty prior to World War II. In 1941, he was made Allied commander in the Philippines. When the Japanese invaded the islands, he managed to hold them off for only so long, retreating onto the Bataan Peninsula before Roosevelt insisted he flee to **Australia**. The army surrendered to

> Integrity is huge with Alpha Males.

the Japanese shortly thereafter, suffering horribly as POWs. From Australia, MacArthur vowed, "I came out of Bataan and I shall return." He never lost sight of this promise, triumphantly fulfilling it three years later. Not only did he reclaim the entire Commonwealth, he enjoyed the ultimate revenge in 1945 when he personally accepted Japanese surrender aboard the USS Missouri.

When you give your word, always deliver on it! There are few traits more unappealing than being all talk and no action. People come to regard people with this habit as unreliable and impotent. Then they begin to look passed them when they need a go-to guy. Never fail to deliver on your promises.

John Wayne: The Duke was such an American icon that when Japanese Emperor Hirohito visited the U.S. in the 1970s, he asked to meet him. Despite never technically serving in the military, countless men enlisted for service having been inspired by his rugged tough-guy image. It was a persona Wayne was interested in maintaining as he got older, insisting that his characters never do anything ignoble, such as shoot a man in the back.

The result was a man with a powerful presence. Part of this presence arose from something simple, something many of us take for granted—**posture**. He never slouched or hung his chin, his back was straight, and his shoulders cocked and wide. It was not something he overdid, just something he did. The result was an imposing presence that commanded respect. A great scene to get the gist of John Wayne and his Alpha Male mindset is in his movie, "The Alamo," where he is speaking to a lady on the banks of a river. It is called "The Stump Speech." Look it up. It is impressive.

Do not underestimate the power of presence. Through body language and demeanor alone, Wayne was always the "baddest" man in the room. People read body language both consciously and subconsciously, and few unspoken things can make people lose **confidence** in you quicker than seeing you slouch at a meeting or give a presentation with hunched shoulders.

President Teddy Roosevelt: nicknamed the Happy Warrior and Rough Rider. Theodore Roosevelt was not only one of our greatest presidents, he was also one of the greatest American men who ever lived. He embodied all the manly virtues and lived life with vigor and enthusiasm. In

> Displays of indifference breed more indifference, while the perception of strength breeds respect and power.

everything he did, he not only talked the talk, but also walked the walk. Teddy's life began rather inauspiciously. He was a sickly child, asthmatic, near-sighted, and home-schooled.

His father, who desired a rugged son, was completely disappointed in him. He would not let Teddy languish in his frailties. One day he took Teddy aside and said, "Theodore, you have the mind but you have not the body, and without the help of the body the mind cannot go as far as it should. I am giving you the tools, but it is up to you to make your body."

Teddy did not hesitate before responding, "I will make my body!" (**Most Alpha Males exhibit self-motivation.**)

From this moment on, Roosevelt become a tireless champion of what he called the "strenuous life." His goal was to live each day with vigor and conviction. He put fearlessness as a constant goal before him. Teddy immediately went to work. He and his father built a gym in the house where he would box and lift weights. He found hiking particularly vitalizing and would climb mountains in all sorts of weather.

He became a strapping and hearty young man, taking up competitive boxing and rowing as a student at Harvard. Even so, after he graduated his doctor advised him that due to serious heart problems, he should find a desk job and avoid strenuous activity. Roosevelt decided to climb the Matterhorn instead. Roosevelt had thrown off his sickliness through willpower and discipline; therefore, for the rest of his life he had **no sympathy for pansies.**

Of his sons he said, "I would rather have one of them die than to have them grow up weaklings." (Total Alpha Male statement. Prone to offending females and effeminate men.)

Teddy Roosevelt brought this uncompromising zeal into everything he did. I believe some of his most famous quotes can help us see the Alpha Male thought processes.

"It is not the critic who counts; not the man who points out how the strong man stumbles, or where the doer of deeds could have done them better. The credit belongs to the man who is actually in the arena, whose face is marred by dust and sweat and blood; who strives valiantly; who errs, who comes short again and again, because there is no effort without error and shortcoming; but who does actually strive to do the deeds; who knows great enthusiasms, the great devotions; who spends himself in a worthy cause; who at the best knows in the end the triumph of high achievement, and who at the worst, if he fails, at least fails while daring greatly, so that his place shall never be with those cold and timid souls who neither know victory nor defeat."

"In any moment of decision, the best thing you can do is the right thing. The worst thing you can do is nothing."

"Speak softly and carry a big stick; you will go far."

"Far better it is to dare mighty things, to win glorious triumphs, even though checkered by failure, than to take rank with those poor spirits who neither enjoy much nor suffer much, because they live in the gray twilight that knows neither victory nor defeat."
— Theodore Roosevelt, *Strenuous Life* (Alpha Male)

Alpha Males like Teddy Roosevelt are molded many times by their trials and the methods used to overcome those trials. They believe that if they can achieve it, anyone with a will can achieve it.

General George S. Patton: General Patton was instrumental in winning World War II. His drive took him places necessary to complete the victory when others hesitated. He let it be known that there was nothing sadder than a warrior without a war! Alpha Males need to be engaged or they slowly die.

Winston Churchill was a WWII hero in Great Britain. His bulldog determination pushed the English through to victory. He also said many things that confronted cowardice and made enemies. **"Those who can win a war well can rarely make a good peace and those who could make a good peace would never have won the war."**

Alpha Male Reflective Questions

Are you an Alpha Male? Do your own self-evaluation. Check off the ones that apply to you right now (not what you wish you were).

1. An Alpha Male provides for his pack.
2. An Alpha Male apologizes instantly. Then rectifies the problem if possible.
3. An Alpha Male is the leader. He does not suck up to anyone.
4. An Alpha Male never builds himself up by tearing others down. He never gossips and never betrays his pack.
5. An Alpha Male's natural element is change. He acts immediately and decisively if necessary based on prior experience.
6. An Alpha Male takes responsibility for his own actions. He never blames others.
7. An Alpha Male is not a liar. He shoots straight and does what is right.

8. An Alpha Male takes on a real fight when it is necessary, only if it is necessary. However, he is not a scrapper.

So What Do I Do Now?

If your desire is to be an Alpha Male, go back over the above check list and begin to work on the areas where you know you need to grow.

Now add these to the list of traits you need to embody in your life:

- Integrity is huge with Alpha Males.
  - ✓ *When you give your word do you always deliver on it?*
  - ✓ *Is that what others would say about you?*

- Displays of indifference breed indifference, the perception of strength breeds respect and power.
  - ✓ Do you display decisiveness or indifference?
  - ✓ How can you tell?

- Alpha Males are molded by their trials and the methods used to overcome those trials.
  - ✓ It has been said, "Whatever doesn't kill you makes you stronger." Name one trial that you've learned a lot from.

Now share this lesson with a young man by tomorrow.

CHAPTER 2

ENDANGERED SPECIES

I have a concern that Alpha Males are becoming an endangered species. No doubt every personality created to *benefit* society can also get out of balance and *hurt* the same society. That is not reason enough to crush the good attributes of the Alpha Male. As a matter of fact, when a society tries to remove what God created, it causes the world to be dangerously out of balance even to the point of being irreparable.

Medicating the Alpha Male?

Testing in our elementary schools for hyperactivity or ADHD is biased and based on what current trends determine to be "normal." The facts are the majority of teachers in elementary schools are female. They classify young men as ADHD and medicate them so they will sit still like their female classmates. Recently, doctors have discovered that a drug called Risperdal prescribed for ADHD causes female breast growth in young men. This is proof that masculinity is being medicated out of our society. (Note: I'm not blaming the female teachers here, they are simply reporting what they are seeing in the children.

However, I am stating that men need to bring this issue to the forefront in our school administrations and even state government before we find that we are deplete of warriors and we have essentially done it to ourselves. One day the young girl students will be women looking for real men to have as a lifelong companion and our nation will be looking for real men to lead us.)

As a former high school football coach having a father that coached as well, I watched him cure ADHD daily. When young boys could not sit still in the classroom, the teachers had an agreement to send them to Coach Watkins' office. Dad would lead the young males outside and teach them how to run and bear crawl. What he knew and I witnessed, as a participant, was that once the young men were able to extinguish a little testosterone, they were more able to sit in the classroom and focus without being a distraction. **A miracle**! **No drugs needed**! This is proof that the best man for the job of knowing and addressing young men's issues is the Alpha Male.

The Lord is a warrior; the Lord is his name. (Exodus 15:3 NIV)

This scripture tells me of the nature of God. Genesis 1:27 says God made man in His image. Therefore, man was made as a warrior, an Alpha Male. An Alpha Male is focused on the task because God assigned the task. Every task has the highest calling to an Alpha Male.

One of my favorite books is "Wild at Heart," by John Eldridge. He tells how his sons would make guns from sticks or even food. I can relate, having raised three sons myself. His point is that most males are wired this way. God forbid that we as a society, tame this spirit that was placed in them. While effeminate men and women may not totally understand this desire in boys to develop the warrior within, do not try to destroy it. One day, you will need this boy to defend your land, your liberty, and your life.

As I write this chapter in the summer of 2014, Hamas is bombing Israel and ISIS is beheading children as well as professing Christians for their faith. Russia is antagonistic to the U.S. with its position in Croatia and Iran. Then there is the nuclear threat and instability of North Korea. Abortion in America is the leading cause of death. Same sex marriage and polygamy are becoming the order of the day because we, as a nation, have neutered our Alpha Male voices on the field of diplomacy. Think about the end result of same sex marriage, no children, no society.

The indicator that a society is on the brink of destruction is when it turns matriarchal in its philosophy, specifically on moral absolutes. Greece and Rome fell when their societies were at the height of embracing the homosexual lifestyle. We need Alpha Male leadership to influence our nation once more. Coach Tom Landry said, "A coach/leader is someone who tells you what you don't want to hear, who has you see what you don't want to see, so you can be who you have always known you can be."

A Fatherless Society

Matriarchal rule is highlighted by a non-confrontational, non-violent approach to every dilemma and every challenge. Mothers are created with a nurturing disposition. Society must remain balanced between a disciplinarian and a nurturer. The danger to our current society is that we are fatherless right now. We are without true male influence.

We are in desperate need of heroes today. A hero is "a man who acts in a moment of time on a need greater than self."

"The only thing necessary for the triumph of
evil is for good men to do nothing."
- Edmund Burke

The Sandy Hook shooting, the Dallas Cowboys manslaughter case, and the Kansas City murder/suicide all have one thing in common. The men who did these things were all fatherless. They had no accountability in their lives. Fathers provide stability for men and women. Fathers are designed to guide, guard, and govern our lives.

Being a male is a matter of birth, being a man is a matter of choice. - Ed Cole

The Washington Times published a story titled, "Fathers disappear from households across America." Luke Rosiak wrote: "In every state, the portion of families where children have two parents rather than one has dropped significantly over the past decade. Fifteen million U.S. children, or 1 in 3, live without a father. In 1960, just 11 percent of American children lived in homes without fathers."

America is awash in poverty, crime, drugs, and other issues. According to Vincent DiCaro, vice president of the National Fatherhood Initiative, it all comes down to: "Deal with absent fathers, and the rest follows."

People look at a child in need, in poverty or failing in school and ask, "What can we do to help?" We should be asking, "Why does this child need help in the first place?" The answer is often because the child lacks a responsible and involved father.

Our nation and our world need men of character, integrity, single-mindedness, and maturity to stand up and begin to reverse the curse of apathy, weak-mindedness, complacency, and cowardice that has gripped this once proud and powerful nation. Only mature men can prevent the following statistics.

> Maturity does not come with age. Maturity comes with the acceptance of responsibility. — Ed Cole

Consider these facts on abortion in America and ask yourself: *Where are fathers in this fight? Where are the Alpha Males?*

- Less than 1 percent of all abortions take place because of rape and/or incest.
- There are over 1.2 million abortions in America yearly making abortion the leading cause of death killing more than cancer and heart disease combined.
- There are over 3300 babies killed by abortions daily in America. Planned Parenthood kills over 333,000 babies yearly by way of abortion with Houston's clinic being the largest in the nation.
- Abortion causally reduces births by around 10 percent.
- Legalizing abortion has a many times larger negative effect on the economy than any consumption-savings effect claimed by some. Approximately 10 million workers have been eliminated by abortion. Of these 10 million, about 5 million would be of age to actively participate in

the labor force today. Without legalized abortion, over 5 million people would be part of the current labor force.

- Legalizing abortion has a massive impact on sexual behavior society-wide. According to the CDC, 15 percent of children aborted were the children of married mothers. The remaining 85 percent of children aborted are the children of unmarried mothers.

Real Alpha Male leadership is necessary to reverse these trends.

- Legalizing abortion increases sexual behavior outside of wedlock. Around 600,000 children (40 percent of 1.5 million abortions), and around 15 percent of the total number of births (4 million) are now destroyed annually by abortion because they were conceived out of wedlock

The following scripture is the final verse in the Old Testament. It's another 400 years before we hear God speak again. This scripture is prophetic in that it holds the key to our fatherless dilemma or curse.

> *Behold, I will send you Elijah the prophet before the coming of the great and dreadful day of the Lord. And he will turn the hearts of the fathers to the children, and the hearts of the children to their fathers, lest I come and strike the earth with a curse.* (**Malachi 4:5-6**)

I am not the only one who is mad about premeditated death. God is angry. He is so angry He sent His Son to destroy it. Jesus, who is the epitome of real manhood, died and took responsibility for my sin before I ever said yes. He died to give me the chance to say yes. He took the ultimate responsibility; therefore, He is the ultimate mature Alpha Male. Jesus led by example. We are called to go and do what He did and even more.

> *"I tell you the truth, anyone who believes in me will do the same works I have done, and even greater works, because I am going to be with the Father."* (John 14:12 NLT)

A Call to War

Sacrificial men always cause a sharpening of those who witness their sacrifice.

We are men who are called to war. God has given us the weapons we need to fight this war for our families, our communities, and our country. The Word of God is the sword of the Spirit. We need to pick up our sword and our shield of faith and get busy doing what God has called us to do. We need to say what God says and lead people into truth. It is the consistent daily efforts that will bring about this change.

> **"Beware of those who stand aloof and greet each other with reproof. For the world would stop if things were run by men who say it can't be done." - Samuel Glover**

There are those like me who have walked this path and are sent by God to lead by example and to father, coach, guide, guard, and govern other men. You can no longer say you have no father. We are willing and able to do what God has called us to do. Each man must decide to be fathered into his destiny.

Who are these spiritual fathers? How do you find yours? What do they look like? He should be someone who has both life experience and a genuine desire to see you personally prosper in every aspect of life. My book, *Take Your Place*, is must reading for spiritual fathers and sons to read and implement in their relationships.

http://www.intensemen.com/resources

Our world needs men who realize who they are called to be and what they are called to do as the Alpha Male.

"So shall they fear the name of the Lord from the west, and His glory from the rising of the sun.

When the enemy comes in like a flood, the Spirit of the Lord will lift up a standard against him." (Isaiah 59:19)

Men, the flood is in motion now. The enemy is trying to destroy our families and our nation. You are the standard that the Spirit of the Lord is raising up to stand against this enemy. The Warrior Spirit of the Lord (Exodus 15:3) now empowers you to stand up, repel, fight, and extinguish the enemy and his tactics. Men, this is your hour to be the hero you were designed to be by God!

*For the earnest expectation of the creation eagerly waits for the revealing of the **sons of God**. For the creation was subjected to futility, not willingly, but because of Him who subjected it in hope; because the creation itself also will be delivered from the bondage of corruption into the glorious liberty of the children of God. For we know that the whole creation groans and labors with birth pangs together until now.* (Romans 8:19-22 emphasis added)

*For as many as are **led by the Spirit** of God, these are sons of God.* (Romans 8:14 emphasis added)

The entire earth is waiting, groaning, and travailing for men to be led by God's Holy Spirit. These are the Alpha Males God designated to stand against the enemy. God is, in essence, still screaming, "Adam, where are you?" Our society is swinging dangerously out of balance.

At the end of the day, the way of the Lord is the only way we will return to a moral and decent society. We need fathers and *grandfathers*, experienced and proven godly men, who can lead the men of our nation effectively. We need heroes who will not compromise the standards of Christlikeness. We need husbands and natural fathers to know their roles, and who will be obedient to God's Word. We need the oversight of a grandfather figure so that if they get out of balance, they can be saved and their family will not be harmed. We need men who will love their wives unconditionally and raise their children with godly character and integrity as their foundation.

We also need women who know their God given roles and are willing to be the helpmate their husbands need to stand up and be the Alpha Male God has called them to be and who will respect and love their husbands unconditionally.

Alpha Male Reflective Questions

The entire earth is waiting, groaning, and travailing for men to be led by God's Holy Spirit. These are the Alpha Males God designated to stand against the enemy.

Ask yourself:

- *Do I know how to stand against the enemy that is trying to destroy my family, community, and nation?*
- *Am I led by God's Holy Spirit on a daily basis?*
- *Do I love my wife unconditionally?*
- *Do I even know how to do this?*

- *Am I raising my children with godly integrity and character?*
- *Do I need training in order to do this?*

Being male is matter of birth, being a man is a matter of choice.

- *Am I choosing to be the man God has called me to be?*

The action steps below will help you get started on the path toward becoming the Alpha Male God has called you to be.

So What Do I Do Now?

- Read your Bible daily to grow in wisdom. Get a Bible translation that you understand and will read. This book is written from "The Father" to you His son and in it are the issues of life. Proverbs is a great book from a father to a son.
- Get a job and a purpose. A man is meant to be gone daily and work, bringing home the spoils. Stay balanced. Go to work during the day, then come home and love your family.
- Pick up a book by Ed Cole called "Maximized Manhood." It will change your life like it changed mine.
- Check out our website for men at www.dangerousgames. org. It will help you connect with men around the world concerning topics related to men. You are blessed to be a blessing. You cannot give what you do not possess. Learn to minister to men in the future by overcoming your own issues today.

- Be a part of a ministry built to restore men like the one at our five star Texas Ranch retreat. Check it out at www. jordanranch.org

CHAPTER 3

WINNING

The focus and discipline of the Alpha Male is revered on one side, while it is difficult to live with on a day-to-day basis. Without a great understanding of who the Alpha Male is and why he responds the way he does, life can be very frustrating living with and around him. For example, can you imagine being married to General George Patton?

Understanding the Alpha Male

The Alpha Male sees life through different glasses than anyone else. God made him that way. He seems to hear a different tune, he feels that there is a higher call to everything he does. He must have order, he must produce or else he feels he is wasting time. He sees no point in doing something that is nonproductive. He is made this way. This may sound a bit bizarre, but believe it or not there is a purpose for men who think like this.

> **Alpha Males will lead others through difficult times when the average leader would fail.**

An Alpha Male is conscious of the woman he has chosen as his mate for life. This relationship is vital and therefore he is passionate about it in every aspect. He feels that she is the primary beneficiary of all that he is and earns with his Alpha Male, sacrificial lifestyle. He takes pride in providing for her at a higher level in all areas of life. He is "The Man" and he is "her man."

Conversely, being his closest confidant, she has a level of intimacy with him that demands total loyalty. She is the one person who has been given access to speak to him in a way like no one else on earth. When this privilege is used constructively, the Alpha Male soars to great heights and she also increases her value in his eyes.

However, intimacy is a double-edged sword. The same mouth that blesses can also curse. If she chooses to forget her role as his chief helpmate, and for any reason chooses to take a critical or judgmental position in her Alpha Male's life, she risks confusing his head and thus turning his heart. How we communicate the truth can sometimes be just as important as the truth itself.

She is in essence either his strength or his kryptonite.

A funny statement with a stinging truth is this: Do you know the definition of nagging? Being right at the wrong time!

An Alpha Male is different in that he sees every sacrifice he has paid to provide for her livelihood and position as a bridge for success. When she disrespects him, his provision, decisions, physique, words, bald spot, etc., his Alpha Male focus and combative nature become initially confused. He cannot compute that the one he has sworn to guide, guard, govern, and basically die for has now unleashed an attack on his character—his very core. If this flaw is not corrected by a meaningful, repentant apology, the Alpha Male will begin emotional detachment, which is not what he or his wife needs.

This detachment is seen as survival for the Alpha Male. It is much like placing a tourniquet on a limb knowing that the limb will probably be lost while rationalizing that you are saving the body. If the Alpha Male continues to leave his heart in a vulnerable position, he is committing suicide. His suicide will leave her and their children unprotected and un-provided for. If he cannot trust his wife to be a helper and not a hindrance to their life and mission, then he must remove his heart from her before she becomes identified as the enemy.

An Alpha Male deals with all enemies in the same way. He does whatever it takes to remove them from the equation. The Alpha Male married her to love her, provide for her, and create a successful life with her, **not** to fight her. It is impossible for an Alpha Male to be intimate with the enemy. So he detaches his heart so she cannot hurt him and therefore she cannot be grouped into the enemy category.

The Alpha Male yearns for a partner that appreciates and respects him. He desires to be the blessing in her life and the knight in shining armor that rescues her. However, his honor will cause him to do the right thing and guide, guard, and govern her even when she has chosen a different path.

I have a friend that found himself in a peculiar position just like this. His wife decided she wanted a divorce even though he had not done anything against her. He was confused, but being a good alpha male, decided to try to continue to provide for her needs for over a year after she left him. When I asked him why, he said, "Well, she is my wife." There is a sense of honor within an Alpha Male that transcends being wronged. Most people just don't get it.

So ladies, when you know you have a good man, celebrate him often. Pity parties, nagging, and berating him are not ways of drawing close to his heart. Be a helpmate so you can be a soul mate.

Alpha Males Are Driven

NFL coaches like Vince Lombardi, Bill Parcells, and Mike Ditka come to mind when I think of these driven men. They seem relentless and have a stare that goes right through you. They see the end of the day from the beginning and refuse to allow anything to get in the way. Read this excerpt from Coach Vince Lombardi's famous speech and you can almost hear the Alpha Male voice.

What it takes to be Number One - Vince Lombardi

Winning is not a sometime thing; it's an all the time thing. You don't win once in a while; you don't do things right once in a while; you do them right all of the time. Winning is a habit. Unfortunately, so is losing.

There is no room for second place. There is only one place in my game, and that's first place. I have finished second twice in my time at Green Bay, and I don't ever want to finish second again. There is a second place bowl game, but it is a game for losers played by losers. It is and always has been an American zeal to be first in anything we do, and to win, and to win, and to win.

Every time a football player goes to ply his trade he's got to play from the ground up - from the soles of his feet right up to his head. Every inch of him has to play. Some guys play with their heads. That's okay. You've got to be smart to be number one in any business. But more importantly, you've got to play with your heart, with every fiber of your body. If you're lucky enough to find a guy with a lot of head and a lot of heart, he's never going to come off the field second.

Running a football team is no different than running any other kind of organization - an army, a political party or a business. The principles are the same. The object is to win - to beat the other guy. Maybe that sounds hard or cruel. I don't think it is.

It is a reality of life that men are competitive and the most competitive games draw the most competitive men. That's why they are there - to compete. The object is to win fairly, squarely, by the rules - but to win.

And in truth, I've never known a man worth his salt who in the long run, deep down in his heart, didn't appreciate the grind, the discipline. There is something in good men that really yearns for discipline and the harsh reality of head to head combat.

I don't say these things because I believe in the 'brute' nature of men or that men must be brutalized to be combative. I believe in God, and I believe in human decency. But I firmly believe that any man's finest hour -- his greatest fulfillment to all he holds dear -- is that moment when he has worked his heart out in a good cause and lies exhausted on the field of battle - victorious.

Are you getting the picture? Do you see yourself here? How about your dad, friend, or coach? These people are among us. They are here for a reason. They are protectors of the masses and placed here by God. You may not agree with their style, but they are here for your good. If you learn how to communicate with an Alpha Male, you will see them benefit your life tremendously.

Understanding the Alpha Male Humor

One way to help you understand what an Alpha Male is as well as how he reasons and thinks is to expose you to Alpha Male humor. Enjoy!

HUMOR: "THE RULES OF MARRIAGE."

1. The female makes all the rules.
2. These rules are subject to change at any time without prior notification.
3. No male can possibly know all the rules.

4. If the female suspects that the male knows all the rules, she must immediately change some or all of the rules.
5. The female is never wrong.
6. If the female is wrong, it is because of a vagrant misunderstanding, which was a direct result of something the male said or did that was wrong.
7. If rule number six applies, the male must immediately apologize for causing the misunderstanding.
8. The female can change her mind at any given point in time.
9. The male must remain calm at all times, unless the female wants him to be angry or upset.
10. The female must under no circumstances let the male know whether she wants him to be calm, angry or upset.
11. Any attempt by the male to document these rules could result in bodily harm.
12. The female always gets the final word.

I have heard these rules and even been a participant in the actual game that these rules are used in. However, a few years ago I came across a new set of rules that were written from the **Alpha Male's perspective**. Please note these rules are all numbered "1" on purpose!

HUMOR: RULES ACCORDING AN ALPHA MALE

1. Learn to work the toilet seat. You're a big girl. If it's up, put it down. We need it up, and you need it down. You don't hear us griping about you leaving it down.
1. Shopping is not a sport.
1. Crying is blackmail.
1. As for what you want, let us be clear on this one: subtle hints do not work! Strong hints do not work! Obvious hints do not work! Just say it!
1. We don't remember dates. Mark birthdays and anniversaries on a calendar.
1. Remind us frequently beforehand.
1. Most guys own three pair of shoes-tops. What makes you think we'd be any good at choosing which pair, out of thirty, would look good with your dress?
1. Yes and No are perfectly acceptable answers to almost every question.
1. Come to us with a problem only if you want help solving it. That's what we do. Sympathy is what your girlfriends are for.
1. A headache that lasts for seventeen months is a problem. You should see a doctor.
1. Anything we said in an argument is inadmissible in an argument. In fact, all comments become inadmissible after seven days.
1. If something we said could be interpreted two ways, and one of the ways makes you sad or angry, we meant it the other way.

1. You can either ask us to do something or tell us how you want it done. Not both. If you already know best how to do it, just do it yourself.
1. Christopher Columbus did not need directions, and neither do we.
1. All men see in only sixteen colors, like Windows default settings. Peach for example, is a fruit, not a color. Pumpkin is also a fruit. We have no idea what mauve is.
1. If it itches, we will scratch. We do that.
1. If we ask what is wrong and you say, "Nothing," we will act like nothing is wrong. We know you are lying, but it is just not worth the hassle.
1. Football is as exciting for us as handbags are for you.
1. I am in shape. Round is a shape!
1. Thank you for reading this; yes, I know I have to sleep on the couch tonight, but did you know we really don't mind that, it's kind of like camping.

All of these are tongue in cheek of course, but you would be shocked at how men worldwide respond positively when I simply read them out loud. Can you relate?

My purpose in sharing these humorous thoughts is simply to illustrate the vast difference in the way men and women think and reason. The point being, if a woman can begin to study her Alpha Male before she is hit with his seemingly off the wall behavior, she will hopefully be able to communicate effectively and not be shocked.

Alpha Male Reflective Questions

What key points from this chapter helped me better understand the Alpha Male?

Who do I see in my life that I would describe as an Alpha Male?

How do I relate to this Alpha Male in my life?

So What Do I Do Now?

Write your own description of the Alpha Male.
Look at the list you made of Alpha Males in your life.

What are ways you can relate better to these Alpha Males?

How would you help others relate to the Alpha Males in their lives?

CHAPTER 4

WHAT EVERY ALPHA MALE NEEDS TO KNOW ABOUT WOMEN

M en and women are as different as night and day. This is true, however, we aren't made to compete - we are made to complete. Like a set of Legos, when coupled together correctly, we just fit! Put enough Legos together long enough and you can begin to build some pretty remarkable things.

Our current world's value system leans in the direction that says you must be the "top dog" to be important. I see a different scenario in marriage. God's Book says the man is the head of his wife - this is a statement concerning order not necessarily value or intelligence levels. God places the man as the head so that he can be held accountable - period. I have met many women that are more equipped to perform certain tasks as well as just being more intelligent than their husbands.

At the end of the day, we must all know our roles so that we can reach our goals. We are a team that has been put together by God. No one has chosen his or her particular sex. Therefore, if we are to serve God well, we must choose to serve in our God-given role.

For instance, Sarah obeyed her husband, Abraham, and called him her master. You are her daughters when you do what is right without fear of what your husbands might do. In the same way, you husbands must give honor to your wives. Treat your wife with understanding as you live together. She may be weaker than you are, but she is your equal partner in God's gift of new life. Treat her as you should so your prayers will not be hindered. (1 Peter 3:6-7 NLT)

Alpha Men, I would like for you to read this short passage again. So many men think that their failures in business, money, or life come from not working hard enough, not getting the right breaks, not being born in the right culture, etc. Consider that **you might just be failing because your prayers are not being answered due to the way you treat your wife!** Remember, she is God's gift to you. You took an oath before God to guide, guard, and govern your family and she is in that family. Another way to remember what men are called to do is to Direct, Protect, and Correct (DPC) as the leaders in families and in society. **Hebrews 13:17** states that we, as leaders, will give an account to God for our families and all those we have been called to lead. Think on that one for a while.

So how are you treating your wife? Is honor a word that comes to mind? Remember, she is first the daughter of The King, *and then* she is your wife. If you had a daughter would you want her to be treated like you treat your wife? Though it is true that God calls men to lead their wife, He also plainly states that when he looks at you both He sees an equal partnership in the Kingdom of Heaven. This simply means that we must know our roles to reach His goals of building the Kingdom of God and saving the lost. We are a team and we hold different positions that were assigned by God and when the team wins, we all win an equal share. **It's not about you!**

Sir, when you submit to God and His will, you will treat your wife well. She should in return respect you causing you to want to love her more. Do the right thing. Find a spiritual mentor to watch your blind side in these matters. Get a spiritual checkup, you need it as much as you need a physical checkup. Lay down pride. Your marriage will improve.

I cannot stress enough how important it is for you to purchase and read "Love and Respect" by Dr. Emerson Eggerichs. The book is by far the best I have ever read concerning unconditional love as well as unconditional respect. In his book, Dr. Eggerichs contends that God commands unconditional love from men because it is not natural. He commands unconditional respect from women because it is not natural for them. The "Crazy Cycle" is a large part of the book and it should be. The "Crazy Cycle" says when the man does not express unconditional love for his wife it causes the wife to express disrespect for her husband which causes a lack of love for him and then a lack of respect from her and so on and so on. It explains what most married couples face in the privacy of their home. If not dealt with correctly and quickly, it will lead to hardness of hearts and ultimately divorce.

Sex

The way Alpha Males approach sex will probably shock most females in that it is very basic, once you understand them. An Alpha Male approaches sex with the same attitude that he approaches life. He is a winner. He expects to win. He develops a strategy based on facts and then he implements this strategy until it produces a victory.

I know this sounds very methodical and heartless, but remember whom we are talking about. He is not your average man. He is a very good man, but the current world does not understand him and unfortunately what people do not understand, they are against. The Alpha Male simply approaches the topic of sexual intimacy differently. The sexual pressure and release for a man is the same as the pressure for a female when she releases words. If she cannot speak her 25,000 words per day she might feel frustrated or pent up. This is how a man feels when he is denied intimacy from his wife. I am not saying this is right or wrong, I am simply saying that if you are married to this guy, it would do you good to understand why he does what he does.

The Alpha Male is visually stimulated. The Alpha Male usually possesses a high sex drive. He is also confident in his ability to complete each task in the natural so it is common sense that he brings this attitude into the bedroom. He feels that he is able to win the best of the best and that would equate to whatever his particular attractions are. For example, if he likes a girl with curves and who is a brunette, he will believe he has the ability to win her. Another Alpha Male might believe that thin blonds are the premier catch.

Regardless of the Alpha Male preferences, once the prize is attained, she is the top of the top and the only woman for him. It is important that you understand this. He believes he has laid down his life for you and your children. He does not desire other women. That day is over, forever. However, he is interested in intimacy with *you*, his wife. When he is obviously in a "good" mood, it should be considered a compliment that he finds you attractive, desires intimacy with only you, and is not running around chasing other women. He is actually in pursuit of you!

Biblically, Paul gives good advice in this area for all marriages. In this context, sexual intimacy actually protects each partner by a sense of fulfillment which stops temptation.

> *But because there is so much sexual immorality, each man should have his own wife, and each woman should have her own husband. The husband should fulfill his wife's sexual needs, and the wife should fulfill her husband's needs. The wife gives authority over her body to her husband, and the husband gives authority over his body to his wife. Do not deprive each other of sexual relations, unless you both agree to refrain from sexual intimacy for a limited time so you can give yourselves more completely to prayer. Afterward, you should come together again so that Satan won't be able to tempt you because of your lack of self-control.*
> (1 Corinthians 7:2-5 NLT)

One common attribute of most Alpha Males is a high sex drive. The same energy that these men exhibit in the business world, they utilize in the bedroom. Another attribute of an Alpha Male leader is that they have an intense desire to serve and please their wife as much as they desire pleasure themselves. It is important to them that you leave the experience satisfied. It is part of who they are. You can now understand that when you are mentally in another place during intimacy, it is discouraging to him. When he initiates advances towards you and is turned down, he will, in the beginning of the marriage, try new tactics. If after a few years he perceives that he is being turned away consistently, problems will begin. Ladies, never be deceived into believing that he is insensitive to your energy levels. He simply desires to be one with you. He desires to connect with you physically. It is his way. This is a good thing.

Take a look at Genesis 2:18 which says, "And the Lord God said, 'It is not good that man should be alone; I will make him a helper comparable to him.'" Genesis 1:26 says, "And God said, 'Let us make man in our image, after our likeness'" (KJV). God is referred to as Father, an Alpha Male and yet we all know He is Alpha and Omega. He also goes by another name, El Shaddai, which is interpreted, "The many **breasted** one."

I have never read a reference for a Mrs. God. Since He has the ability to procreate or reproduce all by Himself, could it be that when Adam was created, he was made in the image and likeness of God the Father? Could it be that Adam was created with the ability to reproduce within himself like God? When God saw that Adam had no helpmate, He said **it's not good** that man is **alone/all one** so I will create from him or pull from him woman.

Think about this truth, God pulled from man a woman and then gave him an **insatiable desire** to **be one with her**, constantly. Every marketing company in the world has recognized this drive. Our world sells virtually everything by using what we call "sex appeal." We sell new automobiles, dental services, hair care products, and toothpaste. You name it; sex sells because God made it attractive. He made it attractive so that the earth would be filled with people. Think of it: two totally opposite humans, created from one flesh, with an insatiable desire to merge as one. This union will reveal God's covenant with His people. What an idea!

Dr. Ed Cole stated that for the man, the procreative process is the most fulfilling and pleasurable process in life. Ladies, the Alpha Male is the highest achiever of all men. Anything he does he desires to do it to the highest degree. Is it any wonder why Alpha Males exhibit a high sex drive? If you watch national geographic, you will see rams, bears, and lions all fighting for the right to be the Alpha Male of the family. The winner of the fight has the right to mate with the females and thus creating offspring with his DNA. The survival of the fittest? Could it be that God desires all males to be leaders and men of integrity, Alpha Males? Could it be that God wants all men to be relentless in their pursuit of Him, courageous in their defense of Him, and intentional in their service for Him? Alpha Males!

Men, your wife is a gift to you. She is to be honored and cherished as God's gift to you for your life. She is not a sexual object to be used for personal gratification. She has emotional needs that differ from yours. Study her. Learn about her needs and desires. As you seek for ways to serve her needs in all areas, you will be served. It is impossible to give and not receive, especially when you are in God's Kingdom. I encourage you to find your fulfillment in your wife and not in pornography. Wives, I encourage you to fully engage with your husband in becoming one when he is interested as well as when you are. This is right and smart.

I recommend a great book by Dr. Edwin Louis Cole called, "Communication, Sex, and Money." You can order it at www.edcole.org under "Majoring In Men." We teach this around the world to men and women and you would not believe the difference it makes in marriages.

Waffles and Spaghetti

If you have not noticed, men and women are different and they think or process differently. Too often what people do not understand, they are ultimately against. This is sad because it is within the gaining of understanding that people mature, grow wise, and become better at and in life. Men and women were created with purpose. We were made to complete each other not to compete with each other.

Here are a few differences you might recognize:

1. Men speak 10,000 words daily while women on the other hand speak over 25,000 words per day! This means that the man usually empties all 10,000 during the day at work, but the woman has around 15,000 when they arrive home.

He is ready to chill out, she still needs to unload. Guess who she plans to unload to?

2. Women think out of both sides of their brain simultaneously, while men use one side at a time. This truth causes women to be able to multitask at a higher level than men. Men tend to laser in on a single objective and often are categorized as less emotional. Here is the reason, when the sex of a male is determined in the womb at about sixteen weeks, the chemical hormone androgen washes over his brain. Many of the fibrous connections in the corpus callosum between the two hemispheres of the brain dissolve. Because of this wash, 80 percent of males utilize one side of their brain at a time. A female fetus does not experience this androgen wash, so she is born with the interconnecting fibers intact. That means most females can restore and retrieve information simultaneously. (Summarized from *Connecting with Your Wife* by Barbara Rosberg, Tyndale 2003)

3. Men's brains are highly compartmentalized and have the ability to separate and store information. Men file these thoughts away at the end of the day: like a waffle. The female's brain is more like spaghetti in that the problem just continues to go around and around in her head. The only way she gets the problems out is by talking about them. Therefore when a woman talks at the end of the day, her objective is to discharge the problems, not to necessarily solve them.

Have you ever looked at the configuration of a waffle? A man's brain works a lot like these compartments. He is uniquely created to place issues, projects, personalities, challenges, pain, and even pleasure into these waffle squares to be dealt with one at a time. The process helps keep emotionalism from clouding decisions and possibly causing the male to make a wrong decision for himself and those he represents, i.e. his family, team, staff, and employees.

A female, however, thinks like a bowl of spaghetti. Have you ever been speaking with a female about her job and all of a sudden she breaks that train of thought and tells you a story about her family? She usually does this without any warning or indication that she has shifted gears or changed directions. She just does it. What happened? One strand of spaghetti just intersected or crossed another strand of spaghetti. She understands completely what the connection is between her job and her family. The challenge here is that Alpha Males do not.

> **Issues within the team arise when we begin to believe that different is bad. Complete not compete.**

She rarely forgets anything. This is good if you have a great past with her. Not so good if you have had issues you would rather forget.

A great team can be formed by two people who possess these opposite attributes. The one brings focus, strength, protection, and prioritization, while the other has great memory, attention to detail, relational strengths, is intuitive, and a nurturer.

Remember this and keep the team focused on its destiny: **greatness**. My wife and I have a great understanding in this area. God has placed me as the President of our home team and she has been appointed as the Vice President.

Her job is to see and hear everything going on in our family and ministry and then to inform me of what she has heard as well as her thoughts on it. From that moment on, the ball is in my court. It is my responsibility to either take her advice or not. Either way, she is no longer responsible for the outcome of the decision I make with the information she has delivered to me.

For example, if one of my children is not making the right decision concerning school, relationships, or things at home, she lets me know her perspective on what happened. I then consider the consequences based on past experiences in my relationship with my son, my perspective as a professional educator and coach, my understanding of the Word of God, and what I am hearing from God at the moment. I then explain my decision to my son and wife, and implement the correction that I feel is appropriate for my child's future success.

Alpha males use all team members to their maximum abilities while keeping in mind that the objective is to win. Men, focus on the game. Ladies, support your men by using your gift, but always remind them that they are "The Man," the leader, and your desire is to follow their lead.

HUMOR: HOW AN ALPHA MALE DEALS WITH HIS DAUGHTER DATING

RULE ONE:
If you pull into my driveway and honk you had better be delivering a package, because you are sure not picking anything up.

RULE TWO:
You do not touch my daughter in front of me. You may glance at her, so long as you do not peer at anything below her neck. If you cannot keep your eyes or hands off of my daughter's body, I will remove them.

RULE THREE:
I am aware that it is considered fashionable for boys of your age to wear their trousers so loosely that they appear to be falling off their hips. Please do not take this as an insult, but you and all of your friends are complete idiots. Still, I want to be fair and open-minded about this issue, so I propose this compromise: You may come to the door with your underwear showing and your pants ten sizes too big, and I will not object. However, in order to ensure that your clothes do not, in fact come off during the course of your date with my daughter, I will take my electric nail gun and fasten your trousers securely in place to your waist.

RULE FOUR:

I am sure you have been told that in today's world, sex without utilizing a "Barrier method" of some kind can kill you. Let me elaborate, when it comes to sex, I am the barrier, and I will kill you.

RULE FIVE:

It is usually understood that in order for us to get to know each other, we should talk about sports, politics, and other issues of the day. Please do not do this. The only information I require from you is an indication of when you expect to have my daughter safely back at my house, and the only word I need from you on this subject is: "early."

RULE SIX:

I have no doubt you are a popular fellow, with many opportunities to date other girls. This is fine with me as long as it is okay with my daughter. Otherwise, once you have gone out with my little girl, you will continue to date no one but her until she is finished with you. If you make her cry, I will make you cry.

RULE SEVEN:

As you stand in my front hallway, waiting for my daughter to appear, and more than an hour goes by, do not sigh and fidget. If you want to be on time for the movie, you should not be dating. My daughter is putting on her makeup, a process than can take longer than painting the Golden Gate Bridge. Instead of just standing there, why dont you do something useful, like changing the oil in my car?

RULE EIGHT:

The following places are not appropriate for a date with my daughter. Places where there are beds, sofas, or anything softer than a wooden stool. Places where there is darkness. Places where there is dancing, holding hands, or happiness. Places where the ambient temperature is warm enough to introduce my daughter to wear shorts, tank tops, midriff T-shirts, or anything other than overalls, a sweater, and a goose down parka -- zipped up to her throat. Movies with a strong romantic or sexual theme are to be avoided; movies which feature chain saws are okay. Hockey games are okay. Old folk's homes are better.

RULE NINE:

Do not lie to me. I may appear to be a potbellied, balding, middle-aged, dimwitted has-been. But on issues relating to my daughter, I am the all-knowing, merciless God of your universe. If I ask you where you are going and with whom, you have one chance to tell me the truth, the whole truth and nothing but the truth. I have a shotgun, a shovel, and five acres behind the house. Do not trifle with me.

RULE TEN:

Be afraid. Be very afraid. It takes very little for me to mistake the sound of your car in the driveway for a chopper coming in over a rice paddy near Hanoi. When my

Agent Orange starts acting up, the voices in my head frequently tell me to clean the guns as I wait for you to bring my daughter home. As soon as you pull into the driveway you should exit the car with both hands in plain sight. Speak the perimeter password, announce in a clear voice that you have brought my daughter home safely and early, then return to your car -- there is no need for you to come inside. The camouflaged face at the window is mine.

Funny, but strikingly real to the men I read it to. An Alpha Male's protective instincts towards a daughter defy the imagination. And we are proud of it!

Alpha Male Reflective Questions

What key points from this chapter helped me better understand what the Alpha Male needs?

What key points from this chapter helped me better understand how the Alpha Male operates?

How does this help me in my own personal relationships?

So What Do I Do Now?

A great team can be formed when two people who possess opposite attributes complete not compete against one another.

Remember this and keep your team focused on its destiny: **greatness**.

Based on what you learned in this chapter, how can you do a better job of keeping your team properly focused?

CHAPTER 5

OXYGEN

A lpha Males are fueled by **respect!** Respect is like oxygen to the Alpha Male in that when he is not getting it, he begins to become irrational and even frantic. Respect is life to the Alpha Male. No matter where he is or whom he is with, every fiber of his being is about respect. If you want to get along with your Alpha Male dad, husband, coach, or friend, be observant of how you say **respect.**

> Wives, likewise, be submissive to your own hus-
> bands, that even if some do not obey the word,
> they, without a word, may be won by the conduct
> of their wives, when they observe your chaste con-
> duct accompanied by fear." (1 Peter 3:1-2 NKJV)

Chaste conduct is respect. If it works on men who aren't saved, just think of what could happen if you're married to an eternally minded man! Ladies, this stuff really works.

Alpha Males take tremendous pride in being the leader. We all communicate in three ways: word, gesture, and spirit. Alpha Males look for honor and respect in all three places. They feel their life's purpose is to get the boat and the people in it to the other side safely and get the "Win." They will not come out and say, "Look at me, adore me, honor me, and respect me." Alpha Males feel it is just the right thing to do for someone who navigated you to the other side.

> **When living with an Alpha Male, remember to respect him for what he has done for you in the past, especially if you are challenged by what is happening in the present. He will be content with that.**

Like Wyatt Earp in the movie, "Tombstone," an Alpha Male feels respect should be given because performance dictates it. The town folks usually become disgruntled with the Alpha Male sheriff once the danger is gone and he expects the regular citizens to abide by the law. He feels disrespected and unappreciated for saving the town from the bad guy because of the way the very people he just saved are speaking to him. Wyatt's wife was seen berating him behind the scenes while every man honored him. Wyatt was attracted to the new woman because she respected him for who he was, and she challenged him to look deeper into his heart and find his passion and purpose. All men are attracted to a woman that genuinely desires to be his helpmate.

Victory Is Important

Victory is important. Therefore, organizing the elements of victory becomes important to the Alpha Male. As a proven leader, the Alpha Male realizes that victory only comes when a team is unified. He focuses on unity and keeping everyone on a team working in one direction. Disunity registers in his brain the same as disloyalty. He must now remove the element of disloyalty that is causing the disunity so that victory will be accomplished. People that are not driven and disciplined to win at all costs, like an Alpha Male, will balk at this action and call him barbaric, unsympathetic, etc. The Alpha Male will simply move on and remove the thing or person that is detrimental to achieving the objective.

Every year in the NFL, coaches and players are evaluated on their performance as it relates to team wins versus losses. Alpha Males get this. If the quarterback is not winning, a new one is given a chance. If the coach is not winning, a new one is hired. All NFL players are Alpha Males as they make up the top 1 percent of all athletes in the world. Like the old adage says, "Why play the game if we are not keeping score?" Whatever or whomever is preventing the team from winning the game must be removed or replaced for the sake of the team.

I was coaching in at Texas City High School in the early '90s when the superintendent and school board decided that a record of 6-4 was not what they desired. The action they took was to replace the head coach with a more successful one. As is the norm, the new coach brought with him coaches from his former school that were loyal and knew his offensive and defensive schemes. Unfortunately the coaches in the old regime were dismissed. Victory was the expected outcome of the new coach as imposed by the school board. He had four years to accomplish this goal or he too would be replaced!

The Alpha Male thrives in that environment; however, the family of the Alpha Male will find his thinking to be confusing at times because our families are usually not operating in this level of competitiveness.

Integrity Is a Priority

Integrity is a number one priority with an Alpha Male. Keeping your word by being on time is a pet peeve of almost all Alpha Males. In his book, "The Remnant," Larry Stockstill says, "When you are constantly late, it speaks of disorder in your life and time. Some people are late because their closets are disorganized; others oversleep while still others over commit and are always running behind. When you are late, it conveys a lack of respect for the one you are meeting with. Dr. Cho told me that if someone is worth meeting with, then that person deserves for me to arrive 15 minutes early."

Integrity is being one with your word—keeping your word and speaking the truth. In fact, in Hebrew the word for *truth* means to be absolutely consistent with who you are, what you say, and what you do. Christ is the *word* and the *truth* (John 1). So an Alpha Male's character and integrity align with the Truth. He does and means what he says; he's a promise keeper not a promise breaker. The Alpha Male speaks the truth in love— often, *tough love.*

When a wife is always late, she is making her husband late. He feels that this is disrespectful. If she honors him, she will realize her tendencies of taking too long in getting ready, and she will make adjustments because she loves her husband and he has given his word. He will never tell his host that the reason he was late was because his wife overslept or needed more makeup.

Ladies, if you are going to be a helpmate, then **be** a helpmate. Take your husband's reputation seriously even if it is only a reputation to his family. He will reward you tremendously. Trust me in this.

Money=Life

Money seems to be important to the Alpha Male. When it comes to money, his life is his time. He is paid for his time. When he purchases property or clothing, food or anything for others, he is very aware that he is giving them his life. Now, when you do not respect the Alpha Male's gifts or purchases, you have disrespected his life. He is not money hungry. He simply relates to the price that was paid to give you your stuff.

When you are consistently thankful for what you have been given, you get along well with an Alpha Male. Keep in mind that being consistently thankful is not flattery, it is simply being happy and being at peace with the sacrifices he has made to give you a way of life that you enjoy.

For example, he comes home from work and you are upset. The kitchen is not clean. The baby has been crying. The day passed you by and you did not seem to get things completed. Your garden did not take and your clothes do not fit. He sees all of this as disrespectful.

As far as he is concerned, you had a desire at one time for the kitchen, the house, the baby, the dress, and the garden. He did his part in finding a way to get these items for you. He laid down his hours (his life) so he could purchase these things for you. Now you are in a foul mood and the reference point is these "things" he purchased for you. The Alpha Male now feels like he has wasted his life. Most men do not mind **spending money** they just resent **wasting money**.

In other words, most men do not mind spending their lives on their wives or children, they simply hate wasting their lives and their time when it is not appreciated or valued. If this scenario becomes the norm, you will find many Alpha Males begin to detach.

I have a friend who saved money for his son's education from the time that his son was born. This savings account was something he was very proud of. It came at a great sacrifice for him and his wife. Periodically, my friend would explain to his son the process and purpose of the account was for his future education. The boy would acknowledge his father's words, but did not seem capable of appreciating his parent's sacrifice.

The time came for the young man to go off to college and the father arranged for his sacrifice to be taken out of the savings and deposited into the proper collegiate account for tuition and books. With great love and pride, the parent's blessed their son with something they had looked forward to for eighteen years. The father would see his son often and ask how school and his studies were going. The son would reply, "Everything is okay, dad."

You can imagine the shock when the first report card came in and only one course had a passing grade. The Alpha Male father felt that he had wasted his life creating this savings account only to be misused. He felt that his son did not appreciate the sacrifice and felt a level of disrespect for his life and its value. The son never said, "Dad and mom, I am sorry I did not study or apply myself. I am sorry that I basically wasted your sacrifice." The son did, however, let the father know when he needed the installment payment on his next semester.

Unity Depends on Honor

Honor is important to an Alpha Male. He understands that unity depends upon honor and unity is essential to victory. People who disregard this component have most likely never been in a leadership position that holds much responsibility. An Alpha Male will usually look up to other great leaders that have achieved much.

> *Children, obey your parents because you belong to the Lord, for this is the right thing to do. "**Honor** your father and mother." This is the first command- ment with a **promise**: If you **honor** your father and mother, "things will go well for you, and you will have a long life on the earth." (Ephesians 6:1-3 NLT emphasis added)*

We have an eternal promise from God, the supreme Alpha Male. When you honor your authority, He will make all things go well for you and give you a long life. I smell the victory here, how about you?

An Alpha Male will take a simple truth filled statement, given by a supreme authority, and live by it daily. He will create a pattern to live by for everything and everyone for whom he is responsible. When it seems that someone who is enjoying the benefits of his leadership decides to live by a different creed, he will address this and not always in a politically correct manner. He understands that their action will cause the team he is in charge of to waiver or falter. The Alpha Male's goal is to get the ship and all of its souls to the other side safely.

To further explain honor the way God sees it let's look at the biblical account of Noah, an Alpha Male.

> *This is the account of Noah and his family. Noah was a righteous man, **the only blameless person living on earth at the time**, and he walked in close fellowship **with God**. Noah was the **father** of three sons: Shem, Ham, and Japheth.* (Genesis 6:9-10 emphasis added)

> "Men want victory, so God gives strategy. When men follow God's Strategy, they will get the victory and He will get the Glory." - Dr. Edwin Louis Cole

Can you imagine being picked by God to save the world? It takes a certain type of leader to do this. Can you imagine having to tell your family God just told you to build a boat large enough to take two of each animal on the face of the earth? If you are married and have children, what do you think your wife and kids would say to you if you told them this tomorrow? What if it took you a year or more to build the boat? Do you think there would have been a few discussions like, "Noah, did you really hear from God? Dad, do we have to work on the boat again today?"

Let's take this a step further. What about the trip? How would you be doing mentally if you had to spend over five months with your family in close quarters not to mention every animal from earth and their waste? Remember, God chose **you** and gave **you** the responsibility to get these people and animals to dry land while everyone else on Earth dies. You better have a great way to deal with these issues because if you are prone to emotionalism or depression, you are done. Compartmentalize the issues and accomplish each by attacking them one at a time, and you will arrive at your destination complete. Yes, Noah was an Alpha Male and God knew it.

> *The sons of Noah who came out of the boat with their father were Shem, Ham, and Japheth. (Ham is the father of Canaan.) From these three sons of Noah came all the people who now populate the earth. After the flood, Noah began to cultivate the ground, and he planted a vineyard. One day he drank some wine he had made, and he became drunk and lay naked inside his tent. **Ham, the father of Canaan, saw that his father was naked and went outside and told his brothers**. Then Shem and Japheth took a robe, held it over their shoulders, and backed into the tent to cover their father. As they did this, **they looked the other way so they would not see him naked.** When Noah woke up from his stupor, he learned what Ham, his youngest son, had done. Then he cursed Canaan, the son of Ham: "May Canaan be cursed!*

May he be the lowest of servants to his relatives."
Then Noah said, "May the Lord, the God of Shem,
be blessed, and may Canaan be his servant! May
God expand the territory of Japheth! May Japheth
share the prosperity of Shem, and may Canaan
be his servant." (Genesis 9:18-27 emphasis added)

Noah got a bad rap because he got out of the boat, planted a vineyard, and became drunk. It does not say he was abusive, it says he passed out. I tend to give him a little grace seeing what he just accomplished could be a little overwhelming to a human. (Ya think?) One son dishonored Noah. Two sons honored him. One son was cursed and the other two were blessed. Do you think God the Father places a premium on honor, loyalty, and respect?

> **"Obedience is God's method of protection and blessing in your life." -Ed Cole**

Noah honored God by doing what he was asked.

The Enemy of Honor Is Familiarity

When we become familiar with our authority, we have forgotten what has been done for us. Without Noah, his family would have been dead. To ever disrespect him or challenge his leadership is to dishonor his past actions and ultimately his God. **Note**: You can always ask questions of your leader, but you should never question your leader's competence or integrity when asking a question. The manner in which you ask is very important to the Alpha Male. He deserves a respectful attitude from those who benefit from his leadership. Alpha Males are not perfect. They will make mistakes. I encourage those of you who are recipients of their great decisions, home, cars, clothes, jewelry, food, time, protection, travel, and love to be gracious in the times when, like Noah, they make unfruitful decisions. Do they cover *you* when you make unwise decisions?

Affirmation Is the Friend of Honor

While it takes a father to affirm a male, a wife or child can definitely celebrate a father or husband. Do this often. You are the people he lives for. He likes to hear that you are blessed and that you appreciate the life that he has provided. You will be surprised to see the more gentle side of the Alpha Male emerge when you practice celebrating what you have instead of complaining about what you do not have. The Bible gives us a great account of the dangers of familiarity:

> *JESUS returned to Nazareth, his hometown. When he taught there in the synagogue, everyone was amazed and said, "Where does he get this wisdom and the power to do miracles?" Then they scoffed, "He's just the carpenter's son, and we know Mary, his mother, and his brothers—James, Joseph, Simon, and Judas. All his sisters live right here among us. Where did he learn all these things?" And they were deeply offended and refused to believe in him. Then Jesus told them, "A prophet is honored everywhere except in his own hometown*

*and among his own family." And so he did only
a few miracles there because of their unbelief.*
(Matthew 13:54-58 NLT)

The King James Bible says He couldn't do any miracles because of their unbelief or their familiarity. You see, ultimately it's the person that disrespects or becomes familiar to the point where you lack honor towards the Alpha Male, that is hurt. Dishonor always disables the one doing the dishonoring versus the one being dishonored.

An example of familiarity is a story that I heard my wife tell concerning a great heart surgeon. She happened to be in the medical center in Houston, Texas and she overheard a nurse talking about world-renowned heart surgeon, Dr. Denton Cooley. Dr. Cooley is famous for performing the first implantation of an artificial heart. The nurse was saying that she could not believe Dr. Cooley arrives in a limousine, only sees patients on a certain floor of the hospital, and is honored like royalty. She had become familiar with him, forgetting that the hospital where she was employed bears his name because of his pioneering efforts in thoracic surgery. Dr. Cooley is definitely an Alpha Male. He needs to be respected. He is a pioneer. He has accomplished great things by taking great risks. He does not desire to be royalty. He, like most, simply desires respect for his life.

Alpha Male Reflective Questions

Alpha Males are fueled by **respect!** We all communicate in three ways: word, gesture, and spirit.

Do I communicate respect with my words?
Do I communicate respect with my gestures?
Do I communicate respect through my spirit?

So Now What Do I Do?

"Obedience is God's method of protection and blessing in your life." -Ed Cole
Honor God by obedience to His Word.
Honor your father- Natural and Spiritual.
Honor the elderly.

Call and go visit your parents, do it now. Do it often.

What changes are you going to make in how you show honor and respect to those in authority over you?

CHAPTER 6

DESPERADO

A great song that describes an Alpha Male's disposition is "Desperado" written by Don Frey and Don Lindsey. I like the Linda Ronstadt version, but the Eagles are not bad either. What person comes to your mind when you read some of the lyrics to this song? You can go to the Internet and see all the lyrics and reflect on how they describe the plight of an Alpha Male and really confront him with the question, *Desperado, why don't you come to your senses?*

The Game Changer

I believe that one attribute that makes the Alpha Male unique is that he approaches every challenge in his life with the same patterns. The many victories he has won have a pattern that he holds dear. He values the victory more than regular folks. The victory affirms him in his manhood and in his value to society. He is his own worst critic.

Romance is a challenge for him. It goes against the norms of war, competition, winning, discipline, and focus. Yet because of who he is and how he is wired, he ends up approaching romance like he does a championship match, with winning as his focus. He wants the most out of it or why should he attempt it? The problem for the Alpha Male is there are different rules to this game.

You see, in the rules of war there is an understanding of honor, loyalty, and integrity. The way men demonstrate these qualities differ from the way women show them. Men understand physical force and violence with each other. We struggle in con-Frontation with a smaller, feminine persona that challenges our leadership, our decisions, and our very manhood. This is especially true when we have been an Alpha Male all of our life.

Alpha Males find it difficult to respond to friendly fire from behind. Alpha Males have no problem finding and alleviating an enemy. As a matter of fact, it is something that makes him feel alive. Confusion sets in when the attack is coming from a teammate you were laying down your life for. It is a definite game changer.

A phrase I have come to understand over the years of counseling and being married almost thirty years is, "It is hard to be intimate with the enemy." When a man feels disrespected, in his Alpha Male brain, he identifies the disrespectful one as the enemy. To disrespect a man is to challenge his manhood.

The first step in developing a great marriage is learning the way an Alpha Male thinks. Most females do not think like this. As a matter of fact most females try to connect with other females by using words. They also do combat with words. This does not work well with the Alpha Male that you have committed to share your life with.

Solomon, the wisest man to ever live, said, **"Better to dwell in a corner of a housetop than in a house shared with a contentious woman"** (Proverbs 21:9 emphasis added).

The word contentious used here means to **contend** for the headship of the home or to fight for authority. A non-Alpha Male will simply allow his wife to run the home to have peace. The problem with this tactic is that she does not want to run the home! She wants to be cared for by a decisive husband, in the long run.

The Bible says the woman is the weaker or finer vessel, which is indicative of her uniqueness of design. She was not built for the daily pressures of decision-making. The man, with his black and white, logical, left or right brain thought process is created for this.

This type of non-confrontational approach by the male is what has turned our world into a matriarchal society and weakened our sons. It creates an out of balance family system. The male gives up on everything now. He does not discipline the children because she argues with him or disrespects his every decision. He no longer does the bills because she disrespects his financial decisions. When it is time for a romantic date, she wants to be treated like a lady.

He has lost his initiative to make decisions because she argues and disrespects his every effort. He has become emasculated and unsure of himself. In the recesses of his mind he wonders about his friends and questions, "Do *they* really like *their* wives?" He is in essence going to the rooftop to get away from the contentious wife. He is disconnecting because he has no answer. If she was a man at least he could "Man Up" and fight the guy. He cannot do that to his wife.

He thought when he married this sweet little petite thing that he was going to be able to take care of her, provide for her, and she would love and respect him for doing just that. He desperately wants to love her and lead her, but does not know how when she attacks his manhood. So he retreats to the rooftop. Unfortunately, he takes his unconditional love with him to the rooftop.

He is then usually battered with more disrespectful words about his non-emotional responses and "running away." This is the same as calling him (the Quarterback, the leader of the house) a coward. This is not a good combination for victory for the family. Keep in mind there is probably no one else in his life that the Alpha Male allows to speak to him in this manner. There is also no one else in his life that receives all of the benefits of his daily decisions except his wife and children.

Wounds in the back always seem more painful than wounds you see coming. These wounds are also deeper and therefore take longer to heal. Once wounded by a family member, the Alpha Male needs to trust again to reconnect. The family member that was disloyal or disrespectful needs to apologize sincerely to the Alpha Male which allows the healing process to begin. If there is no apology or repentance of the action, the Alpha Male may resume his position and even his duties of guiding, guarding, and governing, but the offending party will notice a decrease in the zeal and passion with which he accomplishes these responsibilities.

I had a member share a situation that he encountered with his wife and his daughter. Both instances illuminate how the Alpha Male feels or thinks when he wants to embrace his family, but feels attacked. Keep in mind that in 98 percent of his day, he is respected, admired, and honored for his wisdom and generosity.

> *My wife was aggravated when I arrived home. I could see it on her face. So, I asked if I could help her by washing the dishes. Instead of receiving my gesture in the way I intended, she simply snapped at me and said, "No! You don't wash dishes correctly like I do!" Not sure what I had done but knowing all the signs, I asked, "How can I help you?" - Stone silence. Honestly, I had grown accustomed to her moodiness and mean spirited remarks over the years but for the record, it sure draws a distinct line between the world of work and the world of home. One place I'm celebrated for my abilities. The other place (where the people benefit from my abilities), I'm crucified. I left the home to give her some peace, and honestly to get some for myself, and went to grab a burger. A little while later, I get a text from my wife (yes the one that's giving me and everyone else in the house the cold shoulder) asking where I am. Her next text is asking if I would pick up a burger and then would I go by and get the dog some food! Talk about not wanting to do that! But doing it anyway to keep the*

peace. I never feel more used and consequently detached in these moments.

*My children exemplify similar characteristics when they roll their eyes when asked to help around the house and yet expect chauffeur (Me) service to their friend's house or the mall. I honestly feel like disappearing so that they can be slapped with some reality therapy when they realize Dad's gone and so are his services. I feel taken advantage of but because I'm a man, I say nothing. I wish my wife and children **really** cared.*

Some of these obstacles can be spearheaded from the front. Ask for guidance before you marry and take the advice you are given. The following list is adapted from an article written by J. Lee Grady. These are the women I would tell my spiritual sons to avoid:

1. The unbeliever. Christians should not marry unbelievers. Apart from your decision to follow Christ, marriage is the single most important decision you will ever make. Do not blow it by ignoring the obvious. Put spiritual maturity at the top of your list of qualities you want in a wife.

2. The material girl. Unless you want to live in debt for the rest of your life, do not marry a girl who has dollar signs in her eyes and eight credit cards in her Michael Kors purse.

3. The diva. Some macho guys like to throw their weight around and pretend they are superior to women. Divas are the female version of this nightmare. They think the world revolves around them, and they do not think twice about hurting somebody else to prove their point. Real leaders are humble. If you do not see Christlike humility in the woman you are dating, back away from her and keep looking.

4. The Delilah. Remember Samson? God anointed him with superhuman strength, but he lost his power when a seductive woman figured out his secret and gave her man the world's most famous haircut. Like Delilah, a woman who has not yielded her sexuality to God will blind you with her charms, break your heart, and snip your anointing off. If the "Christian" woman you met at church dresses provocatively, flirts with other guys, posts sexually inappropriate comments on Facebook or tells you she is okay with sex before marriage, get out of that relationship before she traps you.

5. The contentious woman. If the woman you are dating is seething with anger and unforgiveness, your life together will be ruined by arguing, door-slamming, and endless drama. Insist that she get prayer and counseling.

6. The controller. Just as some guys think they can run a marriage like a dictatorship, some women try to manipulate decisions to get their way. This is why premarital counseling is so important! You don't want to wait until you've been married for two weeks to find out that your wife doesn't trust you and wants to call all the shots.

7. The addict. So many people in the church today have not been properly discipled. Many still struggle with various types of addictions—alcohol, illegal drugs, prescription medicines or pornography—either because we do not confront these sins from the pulpit or we do not offer enough compassionate support to stragglers. Jesus can completely set a person free from these habits, but you do not want to wait until you are married to find out your wife is not sober.

Ladies, What Kind of Man Are You Married to?

Is he a good man? Does he treat you well? Does he provide for you and your children financially? Does he keep peace in the house? Does he do his best to make you happy? Then respect him for that in both word and deed. You will find that your quarterback will gain new skills with which to bless you when you use this biblical approach of unconditional respect. You will also find that you will not have to get him to come down from the rooftop nearly as much!

Ladies, as a leader in the body of Christ, I need these men at 100 percent capacity to change the world. You play a huge part in their self-esteem and confident approach to the reversal of evil. Know your role and help us all achieve the goal.

Note: I literally know hundreds of widowed, divorced, and single ladies that have told me and my wife that women need **to appreciate a good man while they have them.** It seems we only appreciate some things when they are gone.

HUMOR: MARRIAGE COUNSELING

Wife: "My husband has no life and he's lost all desire for romance.

Counselor looks at the milk toast husband, walks around the desk, takes the woman in his arms and plants a big kiss on her mouth. He returns to his desk and sits down.

Therapist looks over at the husband and says, "This is what she needs sir about 2-3 times per week!"

Husband looks at the therapist and says, "Great, I'll bring her by Mondays, Wednesdays, and Fridays around 2:00 p.m. if that's good for you!"

Keep your sense of humor. Learn to laugh at your own humanity as well as others. This trick will carry you a long way!

Alpha Male Reflective Questions

Am I a team player?
Am I bringing unity or confusion to my team?
Do I lift up or tear down those around me?

So Now What Do I Do?

"Better to dwell in a corner of a housetop than in a house shared with a contentious woman" (Proverbs 21:9).

Does this describe your household?

What can you do to change this?

CHAPTER 7

HONOR

This article is written, in part, by one of our **female** staff members. She wrote this immediately after receiving a revelation from a counseling meeting with me about this same subject. She is one of the few Christians I have witnessed that received biblical, godly, correction and begin to apply it without offense taking root. When I read this I immediately asked her if I could use it when I wrote this book.

Ladies, this revelation will bless your life if you will apply it to your marriage or to your relationship with your fathers. Remember, this revelation and this article comes from a woman.

We think we can recognize rebellion. It seems obvious, right? They are the kids who kick and scream in the grocery store; the adolescent who slams her door and turns up the music. Or it's the teen who gets drunk, smokes, and dresses provocatively or puts up the hand and rolls her eyes, disregarding your directives. Then we might ask, "What about the wife who spends without consulting her husband or manipulates her husband with sex/favors in order to get what she wants?"

Is this You?

1. Leaky faucet—complaining and nagging until he gives you what you want. [There's a Proverb for that!]

2. Trial Lawyer—out-talking him and shutting him down with your verbal skills [your 25,000 words a day].

3. Blame game—making your husband feel like he is responsible for your unhappiness, anger, or sadness: "If only you were home more, had a better job, didn't treat me like you do...."

4. Clue—expecting him to read your mind but giving little in the way of clues: Sighing, pouting, giving one word answers but when he asks what's wrong, you answer "nothing."

5. Smoke signals—banging pots and pans around in the kitchen to make a point that you're doing the dishes, without actually coming out and asking for help.

6. Water works—most men don't like to see a woman crying so even when he thinks he's right, he'll usually soften to stop the crying.

7. Angling—[AKA "fishing" with bait or lures] withholding sex or using sex to get what you want.

8. Guilt trip—laying guilt on him; telling him how disappointed you are in him or bringing up past hurts.

9. Performance trap—making him feel inadequate: "We're the only ones I know who don't have a new car, etc."

For rebellion is as the sin of witchcraft.... (1 Samuel 15:23)

A rebel is someone who seeks to be in authority, but has not been under authority. A rebel wants power without accountability. A rebel wants popularity but not conformity. A rebel is someone who craves attention and glory. A rebel is manipulative and intimidating.

The Complaints of Miriam and Aaron

*While they were at Hazeroth, Miriam and Aaron criticized Moses because he had married a Cushite woman. They said, "**Has the Lord spoken only through Moses? Hasn't he spoken through us, too**?" But the Lord heard them. So immediately the Lord called to Moses, Aaron, and Miriam and said, "Go out to the Tabernacle, all three of you!" So the three of them went to the Tabernacle. Then the Lord descended in the pillar of cloud and stood at the entrance of the Tabernacle. "Aaron and Miriam!" he called, and they stepped forward. And the Lord said to them, "Now listen to what I say: "If there were prophets among you, I, the Lord, would reveal myself in visions. I would speak to them in dreams. **But not with my servant Moses. Of all my house, he is the one I trust**. I speak to him face to face, clearly, and not in riddles! He sees the Lord as he is. So why were you not afraid to **criticize my servant Moses**?" The Lord was very angry with them, and he departed. As the cloud moved from above the Tabernacle, there stood Miriam, her skin as white as snow from leprosy. When Aaron saw what had happened to her, he cried out to Moses, "Oh, my master! Please don't*

*punish us for this sin we have so foolishly com-
mitted. Don't let her be like a stillborn baby, already
decayed at birth." So Moses cried out to the Lord,
"O God, I beg you, please heal her!"* (Numbers
12:1-13 NLT emphasis added)

Lesson 1: God is Alpha Male and He affirms His choices
for leadership. Do not make the mistake that everyone has the
same position. Honor the authority that God sets in your life.

Lesson 2: The very person that Aaron and Miriam disrespected was the one that went to God on their behalf. The Alpha
Male rescued them.

Korah's Rebellion

Another famous story involving Moses (**an Alpha Male**) has
to do with a rebellious uprising from a man named Korah. The
pattern is the same as far as God is concerned with regard to
the attitude toward order and authority. Promotion and position
comes from God. Watch as God tells His people that when they
dishonor His appointed authority (**Alpha Male**), they are really
dishonoring Him.

*One day Korah son of Izhar, a descendant of
Kohath son of Levi, conspired with Dathan and
Abiram, the sons of Eliab, and On son of Peleth,
from the tribe of Reuben. They incited a rebellion against Moses, along with 250 other leaders
of the community, all prominent members of the*

assembly. They united against Moses and Aaron and said, "You have gone too far! The whole community of Israel has been set apart by the Lord, and he is with all of us. **What right do you have to act as though you are greater than the rest of the Lord's people?"** *Then he said to Korah and his followers, "Tomorrow morning the Lord will show us who belongs to him and who is holy. The Lord will allow only those whom he selects to enter his own presence. You Levites are the ones who have gone too far!" Korah, he has already given this special ministry to you and your fellow Levites. Are you now demanding the priesthood as well?* **The Lord is the one you and your followers are really revolting against!** *For who is Aaron that you are complaining about him?" Then Moses summoned Dathan and Abiram, the sons of Eliab, but they replied, "We refuse to come before you! Isn't it enough that you brought us out of Egypt, a land flowing with milk and honey, to kill us here in this wilderness, and that you now treat us like your subjects? What's more, you haven't brought us into another land flowing with milk and honey. You haven't given us a new homeland with fields and vineyards. Are you trying to fool these men? We will not come."* (Numbers 16:1-14 NLT emphasis added)

An Alpha Male understands order and rank and he honors those above him. He gives honor where honor is due because he understands the system necessary for unity and ultimately victory. He has very little patience for people who do not show honor. Note that when Korah disobeys Moses, he is really disobeying God. It is the same in our families, churches, military, etc.

To be effective in authority we must first be effective under authority.

This demonstrated total immaturity and disrespect for the man God used to take Korah out of slavery in Egypt! Unfortunately, I have witnessed entirely too many instances of this type where the student becomes bigger in his own mind than he really is. Pride is a terrible affliction. I have seen this in athletes as well as Christians who basically forget where they came from.

My father taught me how to respect my teachers, coaches, and especially my spiritual leaders. We will not always agree with our elders, but we should always respect them enough not to dishonor them.

My goal is for every son, natural and spiritual, to accomplish more than I have. I have and will continue to give my life for this goal. Jesus said to His disciples, "You will do what I have done and greater" (John 14:12). The mark of a successful father is the empowerment of the sons.

The student may do greater things than the teacher, but the student will never be greater than the teacher. For without the teacher, the student would not be.

*Then **Moses became very angry** and said to the Lord, "Do not accept their grain offerings! I have not taken so much as a donkey from them, and I have never hurt a single one of them." And Moses said to Korah, "You and all your followers must come here tomorrow and present yourselves before the Lord. Meanwhile, Korah had **stirred up the entire community against Moses and Aaron**, and they all gathered at the Tabernacle entrance. Then the glorious presence of the Lord appeared to the whole community, and the Lord said to Moses and Aaron, "Get away from all these people so that I may instantly destroy them!" But Moses and Aaron fell face down on the ground. "O God," they pleaded, "you are the God who gives breath to all creatures. Must you be angry with all the people when only one man sins?" And the Lord said to Moses, "Then tell all the people to get away from the tents of Korah, Dathan, and Abiram." So Moses got up and rushed over to the tents of Dathan and Abiram, followed by the elders of Israel. "Quick!" he told the people. "Get away from the tents of these wicked men, and don't touch anything that belongs to them. If you do, you will be destroyed for their sins." So all the people stood back from the tents of Korah, Dathan, and Abiram. Then Dathan and Abiram came out and stood at the entrances of their tents, together with their wives and children and little ones. And Moses* *said, "This is how you will know that the Lord has sent me to do all these things that I have done—for I have not done them on my own. If these men die a natural death, or if nothing unusual happens, then the Lord has not sent me. But if the Lord does something entirely new and the ground opens its mouth and swallows them and all their belongings, and they go down alive into the grave, then you will know that these men have shown contempt for the Lord."* **(Alpha males value righteousness and doing the right thing.)** *He had hardly finished speaking the words when the ground suddenly split open beneath them. The earth opened its mouth and swallowed the men, along with their households and all their followers who were standing with them, and everything they owned. So they went down alive into the grave, along with all their belongings. The earth closed over them, and they all vanished from among the people of Israel. All the people around them fled when they heard their screams. "The earth will swallow us, too!" they cried. Then fire blazed forth from the Lord and burned up the 250 men who were offering incense. But the very next morning the whole community of Israel began muttering again against Moses and Aaron, saying, "You have killed the Lord's people!" As the community gathered to protest against Moses and Aaron, they turned toward the Tabernacle and saw that the cloud had covered it,* *and the glorious presence of the Lord appeared. Moses and Aaron came and stood in front of the Tabernacle, and the Lord said to Moses, "Get away from all these people so that I can instantly destroy them!" But Moses and Aaron fell face down on the ground. And Moses said to Aaron, "Quick, take an incense burner and place burning coals on it from the altar. Lay incense on it, and carry it out among the people to purify them and make them right with the Lord. The Lord's anger is blazing against them—the plague has already begun." Aaron did as Moses told him and ran out among the people. The plague had already begun to strike down the people, but Aaron burned the incense and purified the people. **He stood between the dead and the living, and the plague stopped**. But 14,700 people died in that plague, in addition to those who had died in the affair involving Korah.* (Numbers 16:15-49 NLT emphasis added)

Lesson 1: Moses was tasked with saving the very people that were rebelling and disrespectful to him. Why make it more difficult than it already is? Understand God's system and do your part. Do not hinder others from doing theirs. Unify your family. Do not be a part of dividing it or teaching the children to be rebellious. If you dishonor your husband's authority, it is only natural that your children will dishonor yours.

Are you beginning to understand the job of an Alpha Male? You say: "My husband (or father) is not like that." Let him read this and then ask him what he thinks. You will be surprised.

Many people see themselves as being obedient to God, but know nothing of being subject to God's **delegated** authority (those anointed and appointed at home, at work, in church, and in every circumstance). This rebellious spirit becomes obvious when one maintains one attitude towards God and another toward His delegated authority whether they are fathers, husbands, pastors, leaders, parents, employers, policemen, or government officials. We cannot reject His delegated authority by murmuring and complaining on one hand and receive God and His blessings with the other hand. To be in subjection to God, we must subject ourselves and be humbled to serve under His delegated authority **unconditionally.**

> *Obey your spiritual leaders, and do what they say. Their work is to watch over your souls, and they are accountable to God. Give them reason to do this with joy and not with sorrow. That would certainly not be for your benefit. Repent now where there has been rebellion and let us get right and in order with the Lord.* (Hebrews 13:17)

> *Everyone must submit to governing authorities. For all authority comes from **God**, and those in God has placed positions of authority there.* (Romans 13:1)

If we do not appreciate, we will not respect. What we do not respect we will not honor. What we do not honor, we will not obey or be influenced by. When we do not obey our husbands, leaders, fathers, teachers, and pastors we live on a level of ignorance. When we refuse to obey, we cannot learn from these people who care for us. When we live on a level of ignorance, we soon live on a level of poverty because we are in essence walking in darkness by choice.

> *Dear brothers and sisters, honor those who are your leaders in the Lord's work. They work hard among you and give you spiritual guidance. Show them great respect and wholehearted love because of their work. And live peacefully with each other.* (1 Thessalonians 5:12-13 NLT)

Christians, both male and female, must recognize the authority of the Word of God in their lives and in the world—period. The husband/father is designated by God to be the leader of the home. Therefore, he must obey God, lead and take responsibility for the success of his home financially, spiritually, and relationally, as well as planning for the future and the welfare of the family unit in all aspects. The wife must take the biblical stance to support the leadership of the husband 100 percent.

> *As the church submits to Christ, so you wives should submit to your husbands in everything.* (Ephesians 5:24 NLT)

The husband/father is commanded to love his wife uncondi-tionally. He must therefore submit to the Word of God and put down anger or disappointment with his wife and love her and give himself to her at his own expense. The wife is in essence submitting to God when she submits and supports her husband and follows his lead in every decision. Believe it or not, God knew what He was doing when He wrote this through Paul in the book of Ephesians. An Alpha Male responds best when he is supported in his home, work, and life.

For the Ladies

Remember ladies, you married the quarterback of your life and your children's lives. He will respond well to you as the head cheerleader, not as the chief critic. Your quarterback will tend to doubt himself when he is nagged or criticized in the home. Quarterbacks do not perform well on the field when they are not confident. When the quarterback does not perform well, the entire team loses. **You and your children are the team**.

If you are not married yet, here is good news for you! There are many issues that can be resolved before marriage. *Do not settle for less than God's best*. Too many Christian women today have ended up with an Ishmael because impatience pushed them into an unhappy marriage. Please take this fatherly advice. You are much better off single than with the wrong guy!

J. Lee Grady has great insight on the top ten men you should avoid when looking for a husband.

1. The unbeliever. Do not allow a man's charm, looks, financial success or his willingness to go to church with you push you to compromise what you know is right. "Missionary dating" is never a wise strategy. If the guy is not a born-again Christian, scratch him off your list. I have yet to meet a Christian woman who did not regret marrying an unbeliever.

2. The liar. If you discover that the man you are dating has lied to you about his past or that he is always covering his tracks to hide his secrets from you, run for the nearest exit. Marriage must be built on a foundation of trust.

3. The playboy. I wish I could say that if you meet a nice guy at church, you can assume he is living in sexual purity, but that is not the case today. I have heard horror stories about single guys who serve on the worship team on Sunday, but act like Casanovas during the week. If you marry a guy who was sleeping around before your wedding, you can be sure he will be sleeping around after your wedding.

4. The deadbeat. If you find out that the man you are dating has not been caring for his children from a previous marriage, you have just exposed a fatal flaw. Any man who will not support his children is not going to treat you responsibly.

5. The addict. Churchgoing men who have addictions to alcohol or drugs have learned to hide their problems—but you do not want to wait until your honeymoon to find out that he is a boozer. Never marry a man who refuses to get help for his addiction. Insist that he get professional help and walk away. Do not get into a codependent relationship in which he claims he needs you to stay sober. You cannot fix him.

6. The bum. I know one woman who realized after she married her boyfriend that he had no plans to find steady work. He had devised a great strategy. He stayed home all day and played video games while his professional wife worked and paid all the bills. The same rule applies here. If a man is not willing to work, he does not deserve to marry you.

7. The narcissist. I sincerely hope you can find a guy who is handsome. But be careful if your boyfriend spends six hours a day at the gym and regularly posts close-ups of his biceps on Facebook. The man who is always looking at himself in the mirror will never notice you.

8. The abuser. Men with abusive tendencies cannot control their anger when it boils over. If the guy you are dating has a tendency to fly off the handle, either at you or others, do not be tempted to rationalize his behavior. Angry men hurt women—verbally and sometimes physically. Find a man who is gentle.

9. The man-child. If his mother is still doing his cooking, cleaning, and ironing at thirty-five, you can be sure he is stuck in an emotional time warp. You are asking for trouble if you think you can be a wife to a guy who has not grown up. Back away and, as a friend, encourage him to find a mentor (a man) who can help him mature.

10. The control freak. Some Christian guys today believe marriage is about male superiority. They may quote Scripture and sound super-spiritual, but behind the façade of husbandly authority is deep insecurity and pride that can morph into spiritual abuse. 1 Peter 3:7 commands husbands to treat their wives as equals. If the man you are dating talks down to you, makes demeaning comments about women or seems to squelch your spiritual gifts, back away now. He is on a power trip.

If you are a woman of God, do not sell your spiritual birthright by marrying a guy who does not deserve you. Your smartest decision in life is to wait for a man who is sold out to Jesus.

So, here is the ultimate question for you ladies. Do you want to win the game of life? You only get one life, one chance. Throw away all the preconceived ideas of what life and marriage are supposed to be. Look only at what God's word says about life. Focus on His strategy and you will have peace, love, and unlimited success.

Are you married to a good man who wants to lead you correctly and to bless you? Repent now where there has been rebellion and get right and in order with the Lord. Prevention is the best cure. Use this practical application to help you show respect to your husband:

1. **Choose Joy**: A happy wife makes a happy life. Do not use moodiness as an attempt to manipulate your man.

2. **Honor His Wishes**: Give weight to what your husband thinks is important. Do not make him ask twice.

3. **Give Him Your Undivided Attention**: When your husband is speaking to you, make a point to lay other tasks aside, look into his eyes, and listen to what he is saying with the goal of understanding and remembering his words.

4. **Do Not Interrupt**: Even if you think you already know what your husband is going to say, allowing him to say it without cutting him off mid-sentence shows both respect and common courtesy.

5. **Emphasize His Good Points**: Sure, he has his faults (as do you), but dwelling on them will only make both of you miserable. Choose instead to focus on those qualities in your husband that you most admire.

6. **Do Not Nag**: Your husband is a grown man, so do not treat him like a two year old. Leave room for God to work. You are not the Holy Spirit, so do not try to do His job.

7. **Respond Physically**: Do not slap him away when he tries to hug you or make excuses when he is in the mood.

8. **Eyes Only for Him**: Do not compare your husband unfavorably to other men, real or imaginary. Avoid watching movies or reading books that might cause you to stumble in this area.

9. **Do Not Complain**: Nobody wants to be around a whiner or complainer. It is grating on the nerves.

10. **Resist the Urge to Correct**: One husband cannot tell a story without his wife stopping him fifteen times to correct inconsequential details: "It wasn't Monday evening, it was Monday afternoon…, It wasn't blue, it was turquoise;… He didn't ride the bus, he took a shuttle." Do not *ever* do that to your husband—or to anyone else, for that matter!

11. **Dress to Please Him**: Take care of your appearance. Choose clothes your husband finds flattering, both in public and around the house.

12. **Keep the House Tidy**: To the best of your abilities, try to maintain a clean and orderly home.

13. **Take His Advice**: Do not dismiss his opinions lightly, especially when you have asked for his counsel in the first place. Make every effort to follow your husband's advice.

14. **Protect His Name**: Honor your husband when you speak of him to family and friends. Guard his reputation and do not let minor disagreements at home cause you to speak ill of him in public. You are his glory!

15. **Do Not Argue**: You are not always right, and you do not always have to have the last word. Be the first to say, "I am sorry." Be willing to accept the blame. It takes two to argue, so "abandon a quarrel before it breaks out."

16. **Follow His Lead**: If you want your husband to lead, you must be willing to follow. A body cannot function with two heads. Learn to defer to your husband's wishes and let final decisions rest with him.

"He who finds a wife finds a good thing and obtains favor from the Lord" (Proverbs 18:22). Do these things consistently, and your husband will never have trouble believing that fact.

HUMOR: THE POWER OF WOMEN

A couple was on vacation at a fishing resort in Northwest Minnesota. The husband likes to fish at the crack of dawn, the wife likes to read. One morning the husband returns after several hours of fishing and decides to nap. Although not familiar with the lake, the wife decides to take the boat out. She motors out a short distance, anchors, and continues to read her book. Along comes the game warden in his boat.

He pulls up alongside the woman and says, "Good morning ma'am. What are you doing?"

"Reading a book" she replies, (Thinking, isn't that obvious?)

"You are in a restricted fishing area," he informs her.

"I'm sorry officer, but I'm not fishing, I'm reading."

"Yes, but you have all the equipment. For all I know you could start at any moment. I'll have to take you in and write you up."

"If you do that, I'll have to charge you with sexual assault," says the woman.

"But I haven't touched you," says the game warden. "That's true, but you have all the equipment. For all I know you could start at any moment."

"Have a nice day ma'am," he said as he drove away.

Moral: Never argue with a woman who reads!

Alpha Male Reflective Questions

Do I honor the authority God has placed in my life?

Am I refusing to obey and learn from those who care for me?

Am I in danger of allowing my ignorance to lead me into poverty?

So Now What Do I Do?

Take careful note of these steps that lead to poverty and darkness. If you have progressed to any of them, quickly reverse your path and refuse to go this route ever again.

Step 1: If we do not appreciate, we will not respect.

Step 2: What we do not respect we will not honor.

Step 3: What we do not honor, we will not obey or be influenced by.

Step 4: When we do not obey our leaders, fathers, teachers, and pastors we live on a level of ignorance.

Step 5: When we refuse to obey, we cannot learn from these people who care for us.

Step 6: When we live on a level of ignorance, we soon live on a level of poverty because we are in essence walking in darkness by choice.

Give a brief description of an instance when you disobeyed your authority (father, pastor, teacher, or husband) and you now see the results.

CHAPTER 8

ALPHA AND OMEGA

The Alpha Male needs a father. The father keeps balance in the Alpha Male's life. Since the Alpha Male respects and honors his authority, he desperately needs the affirmation of a spiritual father and his natural father as well. I believe your pastor is to be your spiritual father. No other person can or should affirm the Alpha Male. The spiritual father brings tremendous balance to the Alpha Male's life and can help him navigate the treacherous waters between his God given calling, his occupation, and his family. The blind spots are innumerable. The Alpha Male will at some point get out of balance unless he allows a spiritual father to speak into his life, like Colonel Jessup in "A Few Good Men." Dr. Ed Cole was a genuine spiritual father in my life.

The word "spirit," is also translated "heart." A real father-son relationship must be connected at the heart. Why? At the root of this connection, the father will correct the son. This correction is where you can tell if they are in a genuine father-son relationship. If respect remains after the correction, you have a rare but genuine relationship.

Here is an excerpt from the book, "You Have Not Many Fathers" by Dr. Mark Hanby. This portion refers to Acts 16:1-3.

Why circumcise Timothy? Paul preached against circumcision for salvation so why have Timothy circumcised?

When Paul circumcised Timothy, it was more than just a physical, outward sign. Circumcision has always made a spiritual scar--a permanent mark for an everlasting covenant. It was a spiritual operation to cut away the flesh from the heart of a son in the ministry. It is something that must be done by a father in the ministry, so the son can proceed with hearing ears and an open heart.

A son in the ministry must place his life into the hands of a spiritual father. If Timothy was to minister the gospel to his full effectiveness, he had to yield his life to Paul. This vulnerability is an openness to change and impartation. It is a quality of trust that a child has for his father. It is the close relationship of family where problems, mistakes, and imperfections, as well as hopes, dreams, and desires are made known in the security of commitment. The son must fully trust his father to perform the painful surgery in proper righteousness. He must become an

Isaac, allowing his father to bind him with cords and yield to a sharpened knife.

A spiritual son of the house, Carl Mendez, shared this with me and he had this revelation. "God is teaching me many foundational principles concerning the Father/Son relationship. As a son, am I willing to allow my father to cut (correct) me? Do I trust he has my best interest at heart? It's not easy for men to allow their most personal space to be cut. It is through this process that God will fulfill His plan for my life to its fullest. The hard part is that I have to hold still and allow the cutting."

Cultivating relationship with the man you will ultimately settle on to be your spiritual father takes time. Over time you will be tested and this testing will then lead to trusting. This position might be a coach or a military superior; it might be a mentor in your field of employment. However, I personally believe that all ministers need to avail themselves to the men in their congregation at a minimum.

Unfortunately many pastors are not themselves fathered so they feel inadequate to father. This leaves most men in a congregation fatherless and they look for a teacher or another mentor. However, the best choice is a pastor that takes his calling seriously and understands the biblical worldview of fathering, has the ear of God and therefore the tongue of God.

If you are looking for a spiritual father, look for a man whom you respect. Find out how he reacts in a trial. He will not be perfect. See how he has responded to challenges in the past. Does he possess and value integrity? Godly character? Honor? Treat women and the elderly well? Is he a visionary?

The father is the answer to everyone who has already said, "What about the rogue Alpha Male?" No doubt there are extremes in every category of life and the Alpha Male is no different. The equalizer is "The Father." Unfortunately, our world is depleted in this category. Without fathers, humankind has neither discipline nor direction. Take a look at what is happening in our nation and around the world because of a lack of fathers.

Fatherless Stats: 61 percent of homes in the U.S. are fatherless.

- 63% of youth suicides
- 90% of homeless runaways
- 80% of rapists
- 71% high school drop-outs
- 85% of teens in prison come from fatherless homes (http://fatherhoodfactor.com/us-fatherless-statistics/)

Biblically, these tragic results of fatherlessness were predicted or prophesied over 2,000 years ago with the last words of the Old Testament warning us: "Behold, I will send you Elijah the prophet before the coming of the great and dreadful day of the Lord: **And he shall turn the heart of the fathers to the children, and the heart of the children to their fathers**, lest I come and smite the earth with a curse" (Malachi 4:5-6 emphasis added).

We see the results of a world with no fathers all around us. We literally live in a cursed world. We live in an immature, gender confused, wimpy world that would rather placate than confront any day. Where are the Alpha Males? The curse is seen in the statistics I have already quoted.

A chaotic world is now the result of a lack of individuals that guide, guard, and govern us. Fathers were designed by God to stand up for integrity, character, righteousness, courage, honor, respect, and protection.

The Apostle Paul, a Spiritual Father

Look at this scripture written by the Apostle Paul, an Alpha Male who wrote thirteen books in the Bible, spoke thirty-three languages, planted churches all over the influential regions of the world in his day, was beaten, imprisoned, ship wrecked, betrayed, and left for dead.

> *For though you might have ten thousand **instruc-*
> *tors in Christ**, yet **you do not have many fathers**;*
> *for in Christ Jesus I have begotten you through the*
> *gospel.* (1 Corinthians 4:15 emphasis added)

Paul believed in birthing spiritual sons through the gospel and the teaching of the truths of the Word of God. He produced many sons as a way of reversing the curse of Malachi 4. His sons or disciples became preachers of the gospel and traveled the world changing it for the better. These sons were to face the same hardships that their spiritual father Paul faced.

Paul was said to have been "not much to look at," preached a long time, spoke straight and to the point, loved deeply, but was not concerned about pleasing a crowd. He was focused on the prize which comes with building men and raising sons.

I see the frustration on the faces of men daily. Alpha Males that no one understands, including themselves. We watch on television as policemen who have sworn to protect and serve the citizens become angry when they are disrespected. Some even lose their temper and become physical with the lawbreakers. This is tragic but it happens. In most cases I have observed, you see the policeman lose it usually after insubordination by the lawbreaker, disrespect for his authority by the lawbreaker, or just outright slander when the lawbreaker curses him or spits on him. Now it seems the lawmakers are attempting to put more and more restraints on the policemen, which in my opinion will cause a deficit on qualified professionals wanting to attempt this line of work.

I saw the same thing in our public school systems years ago when the lawmakers chose to remove corporal punishment from the classroom. As a public school teacher, I watched as the students began to realize that there was going to be literally no repercussion for their disrespectful actions towards each other or their teachers. The public schools became a scary place for most after the removal of corporal punishment. Was it ever abused? I am sure it was, but instead of banishing this tool, we should have simply allowed mature teachers to use it. We threw the baby out with the proverbial bathwater. Look at us now!

The product of our non-disciplined schools today is no fear or respect for authority in our land. Responsible Alpha Males are the answer. If we neuter them, chaos will ensue. You will like chaos less than an increase in the Alpha Male population, I assure you.

I am reminded of a great African story that helps me explain the power of fathers and their influence on the testosterone levels of males in a society. A certain big game park in South Africa needed to move some of its animals to another grazing area. This was a very expensive endeavor. To cut expenses, the game warden decided to move the smaller, younger elephants first to the other park, thus leaving the older bull elephants behind. Within days the rangers begin to notice that the white rhinos were being found dead.

Poachers were the first thought, but upon closer examination, the rhinos had no bullet wounds and their horns were still intact. Another phenomenon was occurring. The young female elephants were all becoming wounded and impregnated. The rangers set up an infrared station at night to find out what was happening to their rhinos and female elephants. They were shocked to find the young male elephants killing rhinos. They had no idea what to do. They called upon an older game warden for advice. He suggested that they spend the extra money and bring the old bull elephants from the first game park and replant them in the new park with the young elephants. The advice was heeded and within two days, order was restored. **Respect** was the order of the day. The young elephant male gang submitted to the presence of strength, experience, and wisdom. Peace was restored.

This might seem to be too simple for you, but there is an answer for the chaos in our world. It is simple. It is order. God established it so that you and I could live in a blessed society. We have chosen to reject God's ways and walk our own way. To return to order, we must repent of what we did and return to doing things His way. We need some big old bulls to lead the way! Yes, we need Alpha Males formed in the image of God.

God the Father is called the Alpha and Omega. He is the original Alpha Male. There is no getting away from this truth. Study His characteristics and you will see that He is focused, jealous, a warrior, He gives and takes life, He is the leader, and He exhibits every trait we have spoken of in the Alpha Male.

> *"I am the Alpha and the Omega—the beginning and the end," says the Lord God. "I am the one who is, who always was, and who is still to come—the Almighty One."* (Revelation 1:8 NLT)

Begin to look at every movie you see from now on and identify the "father's wound." Movies like Warrior, The Judge, Kicking and Screaming, The Butler, Rocky 1-6, Rudy, Million Dollar Baby, The Rookie, and so on, have capitalized on what the world and the church cannot seem to see. A man or even a woman develops a drive to succeed in an attempt to fill that hole that the absentee father created. It is normally a coach or another spiritual father that ends up filling the hole, and thus healing the wound in the movie as well as in life.

These are real hurts, but the good news is that there is hope. Hope that a man like you will come along and see the potential in someone else. That is what good fathers do; they empower other men with affirmation. Affirmation is addicting to an Alpha Male. The only place we get true affirmation is from a natural and/or a spiritual father.

GF Watkins and Coach Bum Phillips

We need men to be Alpha Males. We need women to help them be this leader. Our world is waiting.

> *For the earnest expectation of the creation eagerly waits for the revealing of the sons of God. For the creation was subjected to futility, not willingly, but because of Him who subjected it in hope; because the creation itself also will be delivered from the bondage of corruption into the glorious liberty of the children of God. For we know that the whole creation groans and labors with birth pangs together until now.* (Romans 8:19-22)

Now look at the stipulation God places on the sons before they can move forward in Romans 8:14, "For as many as are **led by the Spirit of God**, these are sons of God" (emphasis added). God keeps to the pattern of the father leading the sons. The Alpha Male is to deliver the creation.

Alpha Male Reflective Questions

What am I building in my life today?
Am I personally doing anything about the fatherless men all around me?
Am I willing to step out and help other men?

So What Do I Do Now?

Are you willing to father other men with affirmation?

Are you willing to help the fatherless and mentor them so they can in turn be good fathers?

Pray, read the Bible, and ask for guidance daily.
Be observant and look for opportunities with young men where you can lead.
Read Maximized Manhood to get it into your spirit.
Complete the curriculum then look for a place to share it with young men or prisoners, etc.

The next chapter will give you some ways to improve your own life and then begin to mentor and father other men.

CHAPTER 9

FRUIT

M y life has been one with a focus on athletics. My father was an All American with the Baylor football team in 1959. After college, he taught school and coached for the majority of my life. He was my junior high football, basketball, and track coach during the day, and then I went home and experienced life with my coach/dad! Mom was also a teacher/coach most of my life. Dad was, and is, an Alpha Male. He is disciplined in every task to the tiniest degree as well as adamant about his children respecting our elders and leaders. I wish we had more leaders today that taught what he taught.

I only have one brother, Brent, who played all the same sports and was very good at them. He is (you guessed it) also a coach, and a very successful coach at that. He married a teacher who is now a principal. You can say coaching and education is in our blood. So is winning.

Using football and track to garner an athletic scholarship, I eventually earned All American honors in college. I graduated with a Master's degree in Educational Psychology and became a coach and taught PE/Health/English first at the junior high level and then in high school. In the public and private educational realms, I have learned much about human nature, both good and bad. It is easy to see as a nation, we have not created the very best in these educational institutions.

Superbowl Champ Don Davis and My Son Dayne Watkins

We have chosen to make the pay grade of these professionals some of the lowest in the country, and yet they are tasked with handling our greatest and most valuable commodity, **our children, our future**. The Alpha Male portion of the teacher population look for greener pastures to conquer and we are left with people so consumed with making ends meet at home that their abilities to teach and challenge our future leaders is compromised! We need Alpha Male leadership in our states and nation to turn this around. We cannot win like this. Quit paying the politicians millions and increase the paygrade of teachers, principals, and coaches so that our quality leadership positions begin to increase.

My journey jumped from public school education to being a private Christian school principal/coach tasked with obtaining accreditation for the school by the state of Texas. It was at this school and church that I was able to attend a two-year Bible training institute that moved us into full time ministry. I spent the next six years as a principal/coach/minister learning about God and people. What a wild ride that was as well as a great educational curve for me. I felt like I wanted to leave the realm of temporary victory leading football and track teams and begin to lead God's team to eternal victories. If only it was that simple. I had a lot of maturing to do.

In 1996 Rose and I stepped out in faith leaving all friends and family and moved to Katy, Texas to pioneer a church. We named this church Powerhouse Church (sound like an Alpha Male type name?). Within the first eight years, we had grown to over 2,000 members and today we see between 2,000-3,000 members.

After ten years of doing church, I noticed that we were not being as effective as I felt the church should be. I noticed that football teams practiced harder and longer for a game, which had no eternal significance, than the church did. It seemed the athletes were more committed than the Sunday Christians. It was time for a new wrinkle in our game. We needed to get away and solidify our hearts. We called these "getaways" Encounter God weekends/ leadership development time. We needed a place to hold these meetings and so did other churches in Texas. We bought land and built Jordan Ranch.

Jordan Ranch is a $9.5 million dollar retreat center in the middle of south Texas conveniently located an hour from Houston, Austin, and San Antonio that have a combined total population of 10 million people (jordanranch.org). Many have said it is the finest Christian retreat center in the state with twenty-two bedrooms, full kitchen, dining room, and meeting facilities situated on eighty-five acres. In the first five years, we served over 20,000 people including seventy-five different churches, the Wounded Warriors, and the Boy's and Girl's Club of America.

In the year 2010, we decided to create a father/son gathering where men could have their manhood restored. We coupled great men's ministers with camping, cooking over an open fire, and competing in sports each day. We call this event Intense Men and we host it at Jordan Ranch every March during Spring Break. We have seen well over 1,000 in attendance annually. If you are going to preach Alpha Male principles, I believe you have to have corresponding actions that prove your heart.

Our Weapons of War

Today, we don't see men fighting in the streets with swords and shields as in biblical days to establish the kingdom of God. However, we do see men and women fight with their wallets. For example, if you make $1000 a month and then you give $1000 toward an eternal goal, you have in essence just done battle by sacrificing your time. You have given to the building of the kingdom of God one month of your life that you will never see again on this side of eternity. Your time is really all that you own in this life. So, fight with your time by creating finances then giving them for the team to win souls! When we give finan-cially, with the intention of winning souls, we are bringing God's will to pass.

Another ministry that we have been working on for four years is called Helping Coaches Coach [HCC]. This ministry also gathers at Jordan Ranch. In HCC, Jordan Ranch and the Fellowship of Christian Athletes combine forces to reach the 50,000 coaches in the state of Texas with an opportunity to come and be ministered to for three days. The groups are no larger than twenty couples. We focus on three major areas for the coach and his wife: marriage, money, and mentoring. The theory here is that if we can lift some of the pressure in these three areas from the coach, we can help him return to what he was called to do which is help young people succeed.

Our children spend five days a week and six hours a day with the teacher/coach. This is more than they spend at home with you. In my opinion, we have been counterproductive in our church efforts for some time by gathering our church youth on one night per week and preaching to them. The efforts and costs associated with this approach have yielded a fruit that is not what we intended. The statistics of youth that leave the church when they leave our homes for work or college are astoundingly high. These statistics have led me to believe that it would be a better strategy to focus our energy and finances towards helping the on campus "youth pastor" than developing them off campus at a once a week event. The coach has an advantage in that the student athlete is bound to his particular school district by zip code or zoning. The child must attend the "on campus youth pastor or coach's" school, whereas every child has a choice whether or not to attend your church.

A five-year project headed by Barna Group president David Kinnaman explores the opportunities and challenges of faith development among teens and young adults within a rapidly shifting culture. The findings of the research are included in a new book by Kinnaman titled *You Lost Me: Why Young Christians are Leaving Church and Rethinking Church*. The research project was comprised of eight national studies, including interviews with teenagers, young adults, parents, youth pastors, and senior pastors. Overall, the research uncovered that nearly **three out of every five young Christians (59 percent) disconnect either permanently or for an extended period of time from church life after age fifteen.**

> I thoroughly believe it is impossible to *be a success* until you produce successes.

The correct strategy is to help the coach so he can speak life into the student athlete on the campus. To change the campus culture we must help the student athlete. With a 40 percent divorce rate in our students' homes, the coach is the only father figure they may have. HCC is now helping equip these influential professionals by addressing areas that have been neglected previously. If you are interested in learning more about HCC, simply call our coaches hotline (979) 561-8675.

These are the type of projects Alpha Males need to embrace. These are huge impact opportunities (literally, world-changing) that help the Alpha Males fulfill their destiny. I say to you, "Come on in, the water's fine!"

You have heard "you can judge a tree by its fruit." Well, I thought I would let you hear from men that I call sons. Read their testimonies of committing to an Alpha Male system that ministers to the man, but is for the woman and family's sake.

From Dr. Joaquin Molina, Attorney at Law – Pastor, Spring of Life Fellowship in Miami, FL

Dr. Joaquin Molina & G.F. Watkins

Kingdom relationships and connections are instrumental in walking out God's purpose. The elements of honor, obedience, and service cannot be lived out in a vacuum of void and empty words. The embodiment of character must be lived out in a relationship that truly demonstrates genuine devotion and consecration to Jesus Christ. Talk is cheap and a walk is profound leaving a legacy of courageous footprints to follow and imitate.

After several discussions with personal friend and ministry partner Jack King (Faithful Men Ministries), he made a serious recommendation that I get in touch and become spiritually con-nected with Pastor G.F. Watkins.

Several months later, I was introduced to Pastor G.F. and he suggested we meet at a Bethany Church Remnant Conference in Baton Rouge, Louisiana. This would be the first time we would see each other physically, and for some reason I thought he and Rose were an elderly couple but was surprised at how young they both were. After that initial visit we began a five year pro-cess of getting to know the Watkins Family more intimately by speaking often and visiting them several times at their home and local church in Texas. My family and I were able to sense a spirit of excellence, genuine passion and serious devotion for Jesus Christ and God's Kingdom that was worthy of imitating and fol-lowing their example.

For over two decades my wife and I had grown to minister both nationally and internationally with many great ministries around the globe. Seventeen years ago we founded and con-tinue to serve as Senior Pastors of a great church known as, Spring of Life Fellowship, a non-denominational multi-ethnic con-gregation in the Miami metropolis. We continue to minister at both small and large churches and conferences. Our vision is to change the world by restoring godly character in the local church.

Our four children Nick, Josh, Brandon and Christina, also serve with us. Our family began to understand the importance in the Kingdom of God to pursue godly relational connections. The principle to honor and keep company with wise servants of God would have a special promise of blessing and prosperity to our lives, family, and ministries. As God and the Holy Spirit lead you, He will direct your path to become connected with spiritual authorities to manifest righteousness in Godly relationships that will lead you to greater depth of spiritual purpose, responsibility, and wisdom. Upon Jack King's insistence this led to a final phone call. I asked Pastor G.F. if he was willing to accept responsibility and oversight over my life, family and ministry.

This was truly a divine connection, as this step of obedience led to an incredible sense of great peace that opened up great levels of prosperity both physically and spiritually in our lives. This breakthrough led my life, family and ministry to the next level of spiritual ground and authority, leading us to a success that can only be described as God honoring those who honor Him.

As we began to acknowledge, serve, honor, and refresh the Lord's anointed, God was able to entrust us with greater responsibility and our ministry began to qualify for greater opportunities of spiritual service. No one could explain the supernatural exponential doors that opened upon our deciding to take this step of obedience.

For the past three years many things began to take a greater weight of spiritual wealth. The heavens opened up in a special way and spiritual doors and new relationships began to develop.

The challenge to cultivate this relationship with Pastor G.F. Watkins was not without concern. Having become seasoned in ministry relationships we leaned upon God and trusted our lives and ministry to a new season.

Attending weekly phone calls with Pastor G.F. and deciding to integrate ministry schedules would also become a practical reality. Words of wisdom, prayer and visits to our church in Miami, Florida were a true blessing. This was an opportunity to walk the journey of life and share our hearts with another world changing family that would strengthen and help our family and church with greater leadership and prayerful support.

The danger of self-sufficiency, isolation and independent unconnected leadership is Satan's long-time snare leading to great deception and spiritual pride that becomes the downfall of many ministers today. Being clothed in the humility to admit our need of others in the Body of Christ is so important. Not rendering an account and having no one to honor and serve as greater than one's self becomes a sure downfall to many would-be ministers. Submitting our lives to Pastor G.F. and Rose has become evidence of our desire to please The Lord. Our family has an opportunity to show others our passion to serve Jesus Christ by the honor we show in serving the Watkins Family.

The Lord has led us to tithe every month so that Pastor G.F. Watkins can pursue his spiritual priorities and kingdom respon-sibilities to serve Christ with more excellence.

The added blessing to serve Pastor G.F. in events like Intense- the Father and Son conference, Jordan Ranch Vision, Powerhouse Christian Church and The Genesis Team, are exciting for us. We are looking forward to sharing a lifetime journey of serving Jesus Christ to our generation in God's good, acceptable and perfect will.

Dr. Joaquin G. Molina
-World Changer

From Ps. Carven Izaks, Entrepreneur, Pastor of Powerhouse Namibia, South Africa

My relationship with Pastor G.F. came with a recommendation from Dr. Cole. This was a divine connection because not long after that, Dr. Cole passed on to be with the Lord. I was not left orphaned.

It all began with a nervous, yet excited, phone call. I called to speak with Ps G.F. and set up a meeting. The second time we connected was at the Lion's Roar Men's Conference and we were introduced. After the conference, I was invited to travel home with the Powerhouse men back to Katy, Texas.

I must admit that I was very nervous about this relationship as Ps G.F. appeared to be strict, to the point, and a no nonsense man. I felt like I had to be "perfect" and have all my ducks in a row. When I received my first phone call from him, I choked wondering what I was going to say! I thought he was checking up on me and wanted to know how the Christian Men's Network was doing in Namibia. To my surprise, he wanted to know "how are you and how is your family"? He was showing a genuine interest in me and told me that he is here for me and that he is praying for me. I have come to experience this same spirit as I grow in my relationship with Ps G.F.

He is genuine, honest and truthful with a real desire to build a relationship with no ulterior motive. Ps G.F. flew to Namibia twice to simply spend time with my family and me, not for ministry. When I asked him why he would do this, he responded that he values our relationship and therefore feels the need to spend time with me. I came to understand the power of covenant relationships through these acts of genuine love and realness that rubbed off on me. Pastor G.F. is a man who is true to his word. His actions cemented many of the truths I learned from Dr. Cole, but did not quite understand in fullness until they took on flesh when demonstrated through my pastor, coach and mentor.

I will never forget when Ps G.F. challenged me to put on a men's conference for 1000 men in 2004. My heart popped and I felt an apple in my throat! So many thoughts went through my mind and I wanted to give him so many excuses. He said something that opened up the heavens for me..."because I believe in you, Carven." My powerful moment came that day, like with Jesus when God the Father said, "This is my beloved Son in whom I am well pleased." Heavens opened and a lid was lifted. I felt like a lion let out of a cage. I believe every man will experience this when they come into the presence of a Real Man; a coach; someone who has your best interest at heart for you to succeed in every area of your life.

Many years ago, Ps G.F. put the seed in my heart to plant a church. At that time, I did not believe that I was called for "full time ministry." As I have come to know him, his patience, support, grace and fathering has allowed me to grow into manhood and take responsibility for myself first and then others. He loved me and helped me to understand why I was brought into this world and that as a man I have the Ability to Respond to life. It is a choice I have to make and once it is made, don't look back otherwise I am not fit for the job. (This was said during one of our mentor sessions at the gym.) This has been the spirit of Ps G.F.: one of encouragement, lifting up, and pushing me to greater heights. I have known him to believe only the best in people, sincerely wanting them to succeed.

In 2008, I planted Powerhouse Family Fellowship in Namibia, South Africa and three years later Ps G.F. commissioned me. I was ordained as a pastor by Ps G.F. in 2013. In time, he watched, coached, and mentored me how to preach, treat people, show grace, be a shepherd and lead with love. When I travel to the United States, he takes deliberate time out with me. These are the real intense one-on-one sessions that every man needs: someone to do an audit on your life. Every man needs another man in his life (a Pastor, a Mentor) asking him: "Adam, where are you." I will never forget the time he came and met with my wife and I in the lobby of the hotel while waiting for our transport to the airport. In that short span of time, he talked to us about how we handle our money, asked us about our insurances and how we are protected, as well as our plans for our lives. This is the personal interest he takes in men and their lives.

His Example as a Husband

His example has become my model; the image I was to emulate like Paul referred to when he told us how a man should treat his wife. I watch Ps G.F. and the way he speaks to Ps Rose: how he treats her, is always aware of her and whether she is taken care of and protected. He personified for me how Christ would have us treat our wives and when we do that, then Christ takes care of us. I saw how he interacted with his children. He taught me that I couldn't rescue my kids all the time. They have to experience life for themselves as well so they can learn from their own pain and choices. I must be there as a father to support, guide, help and embrace them. He taught me to love my wife unconditionally as Christ loves the church and gave His life for her. This understanding has brought me to maturity in my marriage and my love toward my wife.

His Example as a Pastor

My wife and I have committed to submit to the leadership and covering of Ps G.F. and Rose. We have made ourselves accountable to them. The Lord has led us to give monthly to the Genesis Team (www.genesisteam.org). This covering has brought much peace, protection and anointing. Our people in our church feel safer knowing that their pastors are under authority. As our apostolic covering, Ps G.F. was able to help establish and solidify my authority in our local church and community. His voice has brought much alignment, healing, direction and order to our local church and I believe every pastor needs this structure. I enjoy ministry and having Ps G.F. with me has made the journey and ride all worth it.

Ps. Carven Izaks

From Tony Rorie, Founder of Men and Ladies of Honor, Dallas, TX

I have known and been connected with Pastor G.F. Watkins since 2003. We have served together in the ministry path left to us by Dr. Edwin Louis Cole. I first met Pastor G.F. at Dr. Ed Cole's home-going service where he was selected by Dr. Cole before his death to be the keynote speaker.

Pastor G.F. was a faithful son to Dr. Cole and demonstrated it not only in word, but also in deed. In doing so, he qualified himself to be a partaker of the blessing and remnant anointing left by Dr. Cole. Since the time I met Ps. G.F. to the present, I have observed his faithful and consistent leadership that I can only describe as inspiring. I have observed the transformational effect of his fathering and mentoring in the lives of many of my ministry friends and brothers and the results have been significant.

Leadership is defined as influence and I have observed the influence of Ps. G.F. in repeated settings where men were directed and led into the Kingdom. Not only has Ps. G.F. followed in the path of proven leaders but also he has blazed new paths in the areas of church development, leader restoration, men's discipleship, and apostolic oversight.

Not everyone loves strong leadership, but everyone dislikes weak leadership. There is no weak leadership in Ps. G.F. He typifies the Alpha Male in his commitment to Jesus and his commitment to the development of Kingdom leaders.

Tony W. Rorie
Founder, Men & Ladies of Honor
Dallas, TX

Pastor Frank Manzano, General Manager/Overseer at Jordan Ranch, Schulenburg, TX, Associate Pastor at Powerhouse Church in Katy, TX

Eleven years ago, I was thirty-four years old and my life was a mess. I was a selfish man who only thought about his needs. My wife, Jesenia, couldn't stand me and my kids didn't like me either. I lacked direction and purpose in my life. I was in desperate need of a spiritual father.

In August of 2005, the Lord led me to Powerhouse Church in Katy, Texas. As I drove to the church that morning, I had no idea that I was going to make a decision that would change my life forever. This was only the first step. As a new believer, I needed an example to follow. Paul told Timothy, "Imitate me as I imitate Christ." Pastor G.F. Watkins was the Godly example that I needed to grow in my spiritual walk and to become a better husband and father.

My natural father was a great provider and he taught me how to work hard. I always had a roof over my head, clothes on my back and food on the table, but my dad was not a spiritual man. He rarely attended church and I do not recall ever seeing him read the Bible. I love my dad but growing up, I did not have an example of a godly husband and father and neither did he.

I was at the church almost every time the doors were open. During those early years, I simply observed how Ps. G.F. conducted himself, how he treated his wife, Rose, and how he interacted with his boys. I never realized how important it is to date your wife. Ps. G.F. stated from the pulpit that husbands needed to be intentional about dating their wives once a week or at least every other week. This truly was a revelation for me in my marriage. Over time, my wife and I became best friends and my kids started to like me again! (I think it's even safe to say they love me!)

G.F. Watkins is a visionary and he is always thinking ten years ahead. When we started attending PHC, Ps. G.F. was talking about building a retreat center called Jordan Ranch. The vision of the ranch would be to build leaders and restore families. In the late 90's, Jesenia and I worked for Courtyard by Marriott. I was in management and she was in sales.

When we first heard about the ranch, my wife looked at me and said, "Wouldn't it be great if we were running Jordan Ranch one day!"

I smiled at her and thought to myself, "They are NOT going to let a couple of heathens run that holy place."

In 2009, I felt the Lord speaking to me that I needed to quit my job and help our pastors manage the Jordan Ranch facility. I spent my whole life going after the American Dream. I knew how to work hard and I was making a six-figure salary at an engineering company in Houston. When I heard God telling me to quit my job and go into the ministry, I tried to pray myself out of it! I have never worked for a church or a ministry before but I knew I was going to have to take a pay-cut.

When I first met with Ps. G.F. about managing the ranch, he asked me a few questions: what are you passionate about? Do you want to sit behind a desk for the next twenty-five years? Do you want to make a difference for the Kingdom of God? He was giving me direction and coaching me about my purpose in life. Several months later, I made a decision to quit my job.

At the time, I had many things going against me. I had only been saved 4 years. I was a first generation believer. I had never worked in the ministry. I had never even been on a mission trip! Not only that, but the ranch sat on 85 acres out in the middle of the country. I've never even been to a farm! But Ps. G.F. said that he believed in me and that he would help me.

*Looking back, I see things a bit differently. I had several things in my **favor**. I love God. I'm not a quitter. I have a great wife and kids who support me. I have a great leader, pastor, mentor and spiritual father who has always coached me and set the example for me.*

The challenge in working for and serving an Alpha Male is that I had to re-learn many things. Pastor G.F. is a former high school football coach. He believes in doing most things as a team. I was never an athlete so my team experience was minimal. He is a visionary. He operates in the prophetic, which means everything has to be done with excellence. Serving Pastor G.F. has stretched me and taken me (and my family) to new levels of faith. I stand on Luke 16:12 – "And if you have not been faithful in what is another man's, who will give you what is your own?" (AMP). The Jordan Ranch Retreat Center is not my vision. The Lord spoke to Ps. G.F. to build a facility where leaders and families can be blessed and restored. The Lord spoke to me to help our pastors with this great vision. If I can stay the course, remain teachable, stay away from offense, then God will one day bless me with my own vision.

One of the hardest lessons for a man to learn is how to be second and many times even third! I am submitted to my pastor and will follow his lead anywhere. I don't always understand why he asks me to do certain things but I really don't need to. I trust God and I trust that my spiritual father hears from God. Like most men, I dream of having my own ministry or business one day. But I know that I MUST be faithful in my pastor's vision before God will bless me with my own. My wife & I love Ps. G.F.

& Rose. We are grateful for their wisdom, love & guidance. They have taught us to be generous and to trust in God in all things.

Sincerely,
Ps Frank Manzano

Jose Lopez, My Dad, Me In Piura, Peru

Pastor Jose Lopez, Church Planter in Piura, Peru,

Hello my name is Jose Lopez and I am a pastor in Piura Peru South America. My family and I stepped out in faith and moved to Peru in 2010 to plant churches. I attribute this leap of faith to many things that God has done through specific people in my life. The man that writes this book is not sharing theories or educated guesses. He's sharing his life experience and personal example of commitment to excellence. He is the real deal!

I met Pastor G.F. Watkins at Powerhouse Church in 2001. The defining moment in my life through my encounter with him is this: God used him to give me three things that I needed. I believe every man needs these three things.

1. Identity

I believe most men deal with a father wound to some degree. Without proper identity we are labeled by the world. For so many years I struggled to find identity. I looked for it in the girls I was with, my job, or the things I did for pleasure. Pastor G.F. demonstrated fathering and allowed me to be a son. I'm not his natural son but I have become a spiritual son. God has used that relationship to restore my heart and teach me about my relationship with my Heavenly Father and this has given me true identity.

2. Affirmation.

All men desire to be affirmed. I looked for affirmation from women instead of from a man. Most men reproduce what they receive from the male influence in their life. What I received from the men in my life was passivity, perversion, and absence. I learned from them that if a situation got too hard you should just run away. Pastor G.F. taught me to confront, overcome and never quit.

3. Authority.

I always understood authority as the strongest, the fastest, the hardest, the meanest, and the most audacious. I believe in being the best at what we do but I had witnessed the misuse of authority in my life and these attributes carried negative weight. However, Pastor G.F. models integrity, servanthood, and love. He has mentored me for over 10 years and he has imparted into me commitment, loyalty, and faithfulness. Through his impartation God has positioned me to do greater things.

I can think of many situations where we would all need an Alpha Male leader in our life. One personal example is when I willfully chose to do something I knew was wrong but wanted the instant gratification of my flesh. To be transparent, I would have probably have not forgiven myself, but Pastor G.F. guided me through the process. The situation brought a lot of my past to remembrance and a desire to fall back into the old nature of thinking. Thank God for men like Pastor G.F.! Through a process of repentance, restoration, and reconstruction he saved my life, my marriage, and all those that would someday need me to be an example to them. That's what an Alpha Male will do in your life.

I will never forget when our third son was born in Peru. He died just a few days after his birth. This has probably been one of the greatest sacrifices my wife and I have experienced serving the Lord. Pastor G.F. and his wife flew two days after and were with us through our process of mourning. Their example of availability, faithfulness, and unconditional love marked my life and my family.

Working with an Alpha Male is not for the faint of heart or those who want to skate through life and just live status quo. It's for those who want to achieve their goals and bigger than they imagined. To scale the highest mountains, to run farther, hit harder and be able to take harder hits and keep on going. I remember seeing a sign that reminded me of Ps G.F.: "No Wimps Allowed". It gave me a clear indication that linking up with him would stretch my life and the lives of those around me.

-Jose Lopez

From a man named Pete that was changed then returned to the world and wouldn't receive help. He wrote this letter to me to be a warning to other men.

From "Pete" a former member of our church reflects on his choices:

Pastor,

I first have to say that I apologize. The reason I apologize to you, Pastor, is because I did not follow the good orderly direction that was given to you by God.

I failed at completing the nine books and getting the sword, staying in the Word, being an awesome father and husband. I missed the mark. I was foolish with what God blessed me with. I lost everything, Pastor: My home, my vehicles, my family, my faith, and most importantly my relationship with God. And truthfully, that is all that God ever wanted was my relationship with

Him. Yes, Pastor, when God prunes you and you discover who you are and you have to look in the mirror at yourself, then the truth comes; the failures, the destruction, the loss, the hurt and the dis-belief in God that I caused my family. So I apologize to God, to you, Powerhouse and my family. I send you this email, not for empathy or sympathy, nor money or prayer…no hidden agenda here…but I send this to you as a warning that some man at your church needs to hear that if you don't follow God and step away from your addictions and stop treating badly what God blessed you with (wife, children, church)…you need to turn back, to repent, or you will be like me…all bridges burned, and at a homeless shelter with only my testimony to give…

This man knew to do right. He had the mechanism to achieve freedom.

Here are some other Alpha Males that have been a part of our ministry and impacted my life and the lives of men in our church and ministries.

G.F. Watkins and Case Keenam, NFL QB

Big Tommy Sirotnik, G.F. Watkins, Keenan Smith

Lt. Gen. Boykin & G.F. Watkins

Evander Holyfield & G.F. Watkins

G.F. Watkins and Texas Gov. Rick Perry

G.F. Watkins, Gina & Chuck Norris

Alpha Male Reflective Questions

What is the fruit I am producing in my life?
What am I doing to help equip young men to be good fathers?
How am I helping to change the culture of our day?

So What Do I Do Now?

You have heard, "You can judge a tree by its fruit."

I thoroughly believe that it is impossible to *be a success* until you produce successes.

List the successes you have personally had in ministering to others, especially other men or boys.

Where do you see yourself in the next ten years in ministry? Make no mistake, we are all in ministry!

If you are not involved in an effective ministry, contact the ministries listed in this chapter.

CHAPTER 10

TRUTHS I SHARED WITH MY SONS

It's not the size of the dog in the fight;
It's the size of the fight in the dog that counts.
It's all about the heart!

He must increase, but I must decrease. (John 3:30)

W e decrease so that Jesus might increase. In Judges 7 we see a hero named

> The smaller the army, the bigger the glory for God.

Gideon. His troops numbered 32,000. God decreased them to 10,000 and later to only 300 in a war against a million of their enemies. Long story short, Gideon won and God received the glory.

- Abraham: 318 warriors raised in his home.
- David: mighty men raised in a cave, small in number, large in heart.
- Jesus: twelve disciples changed world.

Alpha Males thrive when the odds are against us and everyone watching says, "He cannot." This power in decreasing comes only by discipleship in Christians. "Go therefore and make disciples of all the nations, baptizing them in the name of the Father and of the Son and of the Holy Spirit" (Matthew 28:19). Go and make disciples/soldiers/sacrificial followers of Christ is a command. Do not make fans or spectators. Build men not buildings! A good soldier obeys the rules. He is disciplined for the purpose of his unit and his commander in chief. This chapter is filled with truths I have shared with my sons.

My Son, Grant Watkins

"Sometimes silence is golden and other times it's just plain yellow." – Dr. Ed Cole

Consider a topic as volatile as homosexuality in our day and time. A man can be arrested for speaking about the perils associated with this choice of lifestyle, and yet this is the type of thing Alpha Males are needed to speak on. Our country depends on straight talk and courage to deliver it consistently. I bring these things up as an example for you to better understand your calling and the desperate need we have for you to go out and fulfill it. We are talking about eternal consequences that if not dealt with today will be out of reach tomorrow.

> "The true soldier fights not because he hates what is in front of him, but because he loves what is behind him."
> – G.K. Chesterton

Only 2 percent of Americans are homosexual and yet their desire has driven them, and their voice has been raised to a level that has caused politicians to legalize same sex marriage.

Here are some statistics concerning the homosexual lifestyle that you should know:

- The median age of death of homosexuals is forty-two
- Only 9 percent live past age of sixty-five
- The median age of death of a married heterosexual man is seventy-five.
- The median age of death of lesbians is forty-five (only 24 percent live past age sixty-five).
- The median age of death of a married heterosexual woman is seventy-nine.

- Homosexuals are 100 times more likely to be murdered (usually by another homosexual) than the average person, twenty-five times more likely to commit suicide.
- The average homosexual has between 20 and 106 partners per year.
- 73 percent of all homosexuals have had sex with boys less than nineteen years of age.
- 17 percent of all hospital admissions are homosexual patients.
- The life expectancy of homosexuals is 15-20 years less than heterosexuals. (Statistics cited by Frank Joseph, M.D. at: http://tinyurl.com/mk4agqc)

I believe God is looking for real men, Alpha Males to simply share these truths because I sincerely believe people are choosing this dangerous lifestyle simply out of a lack of knowledge. Fathers are needed to shake up this sleeping world.

God Uses Small Armies

Small groups or teams of committed people have always moved society. These people die to themselves for the greater good of the team or family. Word and deed are important components of success for a minority to get the victory over a majority.

An influential leader is the catalyst that God uses to motivate the minority to do the impossible. However, the key to the team winning is how it honors and respects this leader. The church influences the world for Christ. The pastor influences the church. Both are the catalyst for change coming from God for the good of mankind. We get to demonstrate the love and power of the

Word of God. Lay hands on the sick. Deliver eternal truth and change destinies. Have the mind of Christ. We are the **catalyst** of this world. We are the fire that ignites the dynamite inside of every breathing human on this planet. Do you know who you are Alpha Male?

Likewise, honor is the catalyst for a leader. Have you heard, "As the head goes so goes the body"? If you want your life to make the largest impact, then you must follow great leaders. You know what makes great leaders great? Those who are great sup-porters, great soldiers, and people who will listen and embrace the vision of the leader to the point that they own it. Where would Moses be without Joshua? Elijah without Elisha? Paul without Timothy? We all begin our journey by following, being under authority so we are qualified to be in authority one day.

The Real World

The following is a graduation speech written by Larry Winget, five-time *New York Times/Wall Street Journal* bestselling author and largely considered to be on the forefront of personal devel-opment and financial planning. These words ring true loud and clear.

> "Congratulations on earning your degree. But the truth is that the degree alone isn't going to be enough to assure your success in the real world.
>
> In the real world, employers don't care much about your degree, your happiness, and your income or really much of anything that has to do with you. They care about what you can do for

them. And from this point on, that's how you have to think. Businesses exist to be profitable. It is your job to make them profitable. If you know how to do that, how to be worth more than you cost, then you have value in the workplace. If you don't know how to be worth more than you cost, then employers will pass over you and find someone else.

Look at what it really takes to be successful in the real world. You have to take **responsibility**. Your life, your results, your success, happiness, health, and prosperity are up to you. When it turns out well, you get the credit and when it doesn't work out the way you wanted it to, you get the blame. It isn't up to anyone else to be sure you are successful. It's always up to you; so be responsible.

Others. Respect your employer enough to be on time and give them your personal best every day because that is what they are paying for. Respect your boss, even when you think he is an idiot because he is still your boss and deserves your respect. Respect your coworkers so they will respect you, and your customers because they pay you.

Clear Priorities. Your time, your energy, and your money will always go to what is important to you. If looking cute is important to you then you will spend all of your money at the mall. If being financially secure is important to you then you will make sure that you save, invest, and live on less than you earn.

It is about **work and excellence**. Regardless of what others may tell you, it's not about your passion—as I know people who are passionately incompetent. It's not loving what you do or being happy every day. You aren't paid to be happy on the job; you are paid to do your job. Success always comes down to hard work and excellence. And it takes both. Hard work alone won't cut it. I know people who work really hard yet aren't any good at what they do so it doesn't matter. And I know people who are excellent at what they do but they don't work hard enough at it to make a difference.

So, work hard and be excellent at what you do. And remember, if *anyone* can do it then **anyone** can do it."

Our world needs straight talk truth in daily, consistent incre- ments to effectively turn around the curse created by fatherless- ness. Will you do your part?

Education reformer Charles Sykes, author of "Dumbing Down Our Kids," speaks at high school and college gradua- tions and shares a list of things that graduates did not and will not learn in school. He talks about how the ongoing feel good, politically correct atmosphere has created a generation of kids with no concept of reality and sets them up for failure in the real world. Here are eleven of his "rules for life":

- *Rule 1: Life is not fair, get used to it.*
- *Rule 2: The world won't care about your self-esteem. The world will expect you to accomplish something before you feel good about yourself.*
- *Rule 3: You will not make 40 thousand dollars a year right out of high school. You won't be a vice president with a car phone until you earn both.*
- *Rule 4: If you think your teacher is tough, wait until you get a boss. He doesn't have tenure.*
- *Rule 5: Flipping burgers is not beneath your dignity. Your grandparents had a different word for burger flipping; they called it opportunity.*
- *Rule 6: If you screw up, it's not your parents' fault so don't whine about your mistakes. Learn from them.*
- *Rule 7: Before you were born your parents weren't as boring as they are now. They got that way paying bills, cleaning your room, and listening to you tell them how idealistic you are. So before you save the rain forest from the blood-sucking parasites of your parents' generation, try delousing the closet in your own room.*
- *Rule 8: Your school may have done away with winners and losers but life has not. In some schools they have abolished failing grades, they'll give you as many times as you want to get the right answer. This, of course, bears not the slightest resemblance to anything in real life.*

- *Rule 9: Life is not divided into semesters. You don't get summers off, and very few employers are interested in helping you find yourself. Do that on your own time.*
- *Rule 10: Television is not real life. In real life people actually have to leave the coffee shop and go to jobs.*
- *Rule 11: Be nice to nerds. Chances are you'll end up working for one.*

In the past, the Houston Police Department distributed a little leaflet titled, "The Twelve Rules for Raising Delinquent Children."

Here they are:

1. *Give the child everything he wants. In this way he will grow up to believe the world owes him a living.*
2. *When he picks up bad words, laugh at him. This will make him think he's cute. It will also encourage him to pick up "cuter phrases" that will blow off the top of your head later.*
3. *Never give him any spiritual training. Wait until he is twenty-one, and then let him "decide for himself."*
4. *Avoid the use of the word "wrong." It may develop a guilt complex. This will condition him to believe later, when he is arrested for stealing a car, that society is against him and he is being persecuted.*
5. *Pick up everything he leaves lying around—books, shoes, and clothes. Do everything for him so that he will be experienced in throwing all responsibility on others.*
6. *Let him read any printed matter he can get his hands on. Be careful that the silverware and drinking glasses*

are sterilized, but don't worry about his mind feasting on garbage.

7. *Quarrel frequently in the presence of your children. In this way they will not be too shocked when the home is broken up later.*

8. *Give the child all the spending money he wants. Never let him earn his. Why should he have things as tough as you did?*

9. *Satisfy his every craving for food, drink, and comfort. See that every sensual desire is gratified. Denial may lead to harmful frustration.*

10. *Take his part against neighbors, teachers, and policemen. They are all prejudiced against your child.*

11. *When he gets into real trouble, apologize to yourself by saying, "I never could do anything with him!"*

12. *Prepare yourself for a life of grief. You'll surely have it.*

I thought you might enjoy this interesting prayer given in Kansas at the opening session of their House. It seems that prayer still upsets people. When Minister Joe Wright was asked to open the new session of the Kansas House, everyone was expecting the usual generalities, but this is what they heard:

Heavenly Father,

We come before You today to ask Your forgiveness and seek your direction and guidance. We know Your Word says, "Woe to those who call evil good," but that's exactly what we have done. We have lost our Spiritual equilibrium and inverted our values. We confess that; we have ridiculed the absolute truth of Your

Word and called it pluralism; We have worshipped other gods and called it multiculturalism; We have endorsed perversion and called it an alternative lifestyle; We have exploited the poor and called it the lottery; We have neglected the needy and called it self-preservation; We have rewarded laziness and called it welfare; We have killed our unborn and called it choice; We have shot abortionists and called it justifiable; We have neglected to discipline our children and called it building self-esteem; We have abused power and called it political savvy; We have coveted our neighbor's possessions and called it ambition; We have polluted the air with profanity and pornography and called it freedom of expression; We have ridiculed the time-honored values of our forefathers and called it enlightenment. Search us, O God, and know our hearts today; try us and see if there be some wicked way in us; cleanse us from every sin and set us free. Guide and bless these men and women who have been sent here by the people of this state and who have been ordained by You, to govern this great state of Kansas. Grant them your wisdom to rule and may their decisions direct us to the center of Your Will.

Wow, what if every man and woman reading this book were to look for opportunities to speak truth in board rooms, classrooms, and kitchen tables? I am convinced change would occur. Just let the Word do the work!

The following statements are attributed to Winston Churchill:

- "An appeaser is one who feeds a crocodile – hoping it will eat him last."

- "A lie gets halfway around the world before the truth has a chance to get its pants on."
- "Once in a while you will stumble upon the truth but most of us manage to pick ourselves up and hurry along as if nothing had happened."
- "If you are going to go through hell, keep going."
- "History will be kind to me for I intend to write it."
- "The truth is incontrovertible, malice may attack it, ignorance may deride it, but in the end, there it is."
- "A pessimist sees the difficulty in every opportunity; an optimist sees the opportunity in every difficulty."
- "To improve is to change; to be perfect is to change often."
- "Success consists of going from failure to failure without loss of enthusiasm."
- "Courage is the first of human qualities because it is the quality that guarantees all the others."
- "The problems of victory are more agreeable than those of defeat, but they are not less difficult."
- "If you will not fight for right when you can easily win without bloodshed; if you will not fight when your victory is sure and not too costly; you may come to the moment when you will have to fight with all the odds against you and only a precarious chance of survival. There may even be a worse case. You may have to fight when there is no hope of victory, because it is better to perish than to live as slaves."

I have included these truths so you will have an idea of what to say and you will be ready when invited to speak. Be courageous, Alpha Male!

"The longer I live, the more I realize the impact of attitude on life. Attitude, to me, is more important than facts. It is more important than the past, than education, than money, than circumstances, than failures, than successes, than what other people think or say or do. It is more important than appearance, talent, or skill. It will make or break a company...a church...a home. The remarkable thing is we have a choice every day regarding the attitude we will embrace for that day. We cannot change our past...we cannot change the fact that people will act in a certain way. We cannot change the inevitable. The only thing we can do is play with the one string we have, and that is our attitude...I am convinced that life is 10 percent what happens to me and 90 percent how I react to it. And so it is with you...we are in charge of our attitudes!"
- **Charles Swindoll**

Hero: One who acts in a moment of time on a need greater than self.

Dr. David Livingston was a Scottish missionary during the mid-1800s. He sailed to Africa to spread the Good News of salvation through Jesus Christ to a people who had never heard. The Missionary Society that sent him wrote him and said, "If you will pave a road from the coast to where you are inland, we will send men to help you." Livingston replied, "If the men you desire to send need a road before they will come, I don't need them!"

In a speech to Cambridge University students he also said, "People talk of the sacrifice I have made in spending so much of my life in Africa. Can that be called a sacrifice, which is simply paid back as a small part of a great debt owing to our God, which we can never repay? Is that a sacrifice, which brings its own blest reward in healthful activity, the consciousness of doing good, peace of mind, and a bright hope of a glorious destiny hereafter? Away with the word in such a view and with such a thought! It is emphatically no sacrifice. Say rather it is a privilege. Anxiety, sickness, suffering, or danger now and then with a foregoing of the common conveniences and charities of this life, may make us pause and cause the spirit to waver and the soul to sink; but let this only be for a moment. All these are nothing when compared with the glory, which shall be revealed in and for us. I never made a sacrifice."

With great risk and sacrifice comes great reward, which is saved for only the brave. Listen to his description of an African waterfall and keep in mind no European had ever seen or written of this sight:

> *No one can imagine the beauty of the view from anything witnessed in England. European eyes had never seen it before; but angels in their flight must have gazed upon scenes so lovely.*

That my friends is called reward! How about you? Why do you do what you do? The more you give of your life, the more you will receive. Quit waiting!

Alpha Male Reflective Questions

Do I know who I am?
Why do I do what I do?
What am I waiting for?

So What Do I Do Now?

Have you heard, "As the head goes so goes the body"? If you want your life to make the largest impact, then you must follow great leaders.

Who are the leaders you have chosen to follow?

You know what makes great leaders great? Great supporters, great soldiers; people who will listen and embrace the vision of the leader to the point that they own it.

Where can you be a great supporter and soldier?

CHAPTER 11

SACRIFICE GOES WITH THE TERRITORY

T hose of us who live in the West are poised at the outset of the greatest wealth transfer in history.

In the United States alone, the "greatest generation"—those born between 1910 and 1940 whose industriousness generated incredible amounts of wealth—is **transferring their last $12 trillion** to their heirs. Over the next twenty-five to forty years, the baby boomer generation will transfer between **$30 trillion** and **$136 trillion** to their heirs—not to mention the additional wealth that will be generated during this time. Where will all this money go?

> *If then you have not been faithful in the unrighteous wealth, who will entrust to you the true riches?* **(Luke 16:11)**

We are accustomed to the biblical message that we should trust God. Here is another thought, does God trust *us*? If we are not faithful with money, which is unrighteous and not worth much, then who will entrust to us the true riches of spiritual wealth and power?

Today we pray for revival, but are we living lives of **radical generosity** in the same manner that our forebears did? Put another way, **is true revival stifled by our comfort and affluence?**

When I describe radical generosity, I am talking about joyfully giving all of one's time, talent, and treasures for the sake of God's kingdom and a heavenly reward is all that is expected as his return on investment. **This is an attribute of an Alpha Male**. We look at giving to God's work as an offensive weapon. When a man goes to work, he earns a paycheck. He is paid for his time and knowledge of which he invests a portion into the fight against evil. He understands the dynamics of synergy and how a corporate body can do much more than an individual so he utilizes his church as a means to invest in God and do war against evil! Remember, he lives for the chance to do war, war comes with sacrifice, to compete, and to win.

Examples of Radical Generosity

He used his wealth as a sword to cut down evil and to build eternal equity!

In the 20th century, **R. G. LeTourneau** (1888-1969) committed his life to Christ at a revival in 1904 at the age of sixteen. He went on to become a successful businessman and the father of the modern earthmoving industry. As his wealth increased, he committed to living on just 10 percent of his income. He gave away 90 percent of both his personal income and corporate profits to kingdom work.

Not only did he found LeTourneau University in Texas, but he also gave generously to mission work in Africa and South America—radical generosity that helped resource the 20th-century explosion of Christianity in the Global South.

When asked about his commitment to give so much away, LeTourneau answered, "The question is not how much of my money I give to God, but rather how much of God's money I keep for myself." R.G. LeTourneau was a great example of an Alpha Male.

In the 18th century, **John Wesley** (1703-1791) was a towering figure in the Evangelical Awakening in England. His tireless teaching, preaching, writing, organizing, and activism are without parallel in his day. His book sales alone earned him more than £100,000 (about **$10 million today**) in his lifetime, yet he died penniless—having given nearly all his resources to the poor, Christian causes, and the ministry of others.

> His time, talent, and treasure were all radically laid on the altar of God's kingdom-building work.

Today, on the cusp of the largest wealth exchange in history, what might it look like to follow in the footsteps of these generous forebears? Interestingly, I think one of the most helpful formulations remains Wesley's famous sermon, "The Use of Money" which is an extended examination of Luke 16:9. The entire sermon bears reading, and I have been thinking what our world might look like if God gave us courage to live out these words from the sermon's conclusion:

"Gain all you can, without hurting either yourself or your neighbor in soul or body, by applying hereto

with unintermitted diligence, and with all the under-standing which God has given you; save all you can, by cutting off every expense which serves only to indulge foolish desire; to gratify either the desire of flesh, the desire of the eye, or the pride of life; waste nothing, living or dying, on sin or folly, whether for yourself or your children; and then, give all you can, or, in other words, give all you have to God. Do not stint yourself . . . to this or that proportion. **"Render unto God," not a tenth, not a third, not half, but all that is God's, be it more or less; by employing all on yourself, your household, the household of faith, and all mankind, in such a manner, that you may give a good account of your stewardship when ye can be no longer stewards."**

While radical generosity in each Christian's life and context will look different, it will always cause our lives to look radically different from our unbelieving neighbors. C.S. Lewis' words on Christian giving should strike a chord in all of our affluent hearts. He writes:

I do not believe one can settle how much we ought to give. I am afraid the only safe rule is to give more than we can spare. In other words, if our expen-diture on comforts, luxuries, amusements, etc., is up to the standard common among those with the same income as our own, we are probably giving away too little. If our charities do not at all pinch or hamper us, I should say they [our expenditures] are too small. There ought to be things we should like to do and cannot do because our charities expenditure excludes them. (Mere Christianity, 87)

Today we are quick to pray for revival in our land. May we, in this vapor of a life, be joyfully pinched and hampered as we lay up treasure in heaven, our true home purchased for us by Christ at the cross. As we keep our eyes fixed on Christ, God just may use us, and the greatest wealth transfer in history, to— once again—turn the world upside down (Acts 17:6).

To turn our country around, we need more Christ led Alpha Males in every area of our country's leadership from politics, to education, to the pulpits. We need courageous men to speak out against current cultural norms that have been allowed by our matriarchal society. **Adam, where are you?**

> *"You have enemies? Good. That means you've stood up for something, sometime in your life."*
> **- Winston Churchill**

The facts are that we have a subculture in American churches today that are not exhibiting Christ's characteristics when it comes to giving sacrificially. This needs to be changed if we are to overcome the spiritual mediocrity of our current church culture. Statistics say that of every declared born again believer, only 4 percent give 10 percent or more to ministry efforts. This means that the majority of confessing believers do not believe enough in the great commission to invest 10 percent of their incomes to winning souls. When I read this a righteous indignation rises inside me. It reminds me of my football coaching days when we always had some of the team that didn't want to sacrifice, give their all in practice, but sure wanted to suit up on Friday nights. They wanted all the reward but none of the sacrifice. They were takers not givers. If I, as a mortal man, could discern the intent of these football players hearts, do you not think God who made the heavens and the earth can discern the intentions of our hearts when we make silly excuses as to why we do not sacrifice for souls?

> **Sacrifice and commitment are two words that describe the Alpha Male.**

I personally believe that God set up a system to feed the hungry and shelter the homeless, and most importantly save the lost in the very beginning of His instruction manual called the Bible.

*"**For I am the Lord, I do not change;** therefore you are not consumed, O sons of Jacob. Yet from the days of **your fathers,** you have gone away from My ordinances and have not kept them. Return to Me, and I will return to you," says the Lord of hosts. "But you said, 'In what way shall we return?' Will a man **rob God**? Yet you have robbed Me! But you say, 'In what way have we robbed You?' **In tithes** and offerings. You are cursed with a curse, for you have robbed Me, even this whole nation. Bring all the tithes into the storehouse, that there*

> may be **food in My house**, and try Me now in this," says the Lord of Hosts, "If I will not open for you the windows of heaven and pour out for you **such blessing** that there will **not be room** enough to receive it. And I will rebuke the devourer for your sakes, so that he will not destroy the fruit of your ground, nor shall the vine fail to bear fruit for you in the field," says the Lord of hosts; **And all nations will call you blessed, for you will be a delightful land,"** says the Lord of hosts. (Malachi 3:6-12 emphasis added)

The word tithe here is speaking about the first 10 percent of a family's income. God gives us everything we own from our breath to our children to our income. He basically says here that if we value (appreciate) Him, we will honor Him with the Holy Thing called the 10 percent (tithe) by returning it so that it can be used as a means to save others. Unbelievers do not tithe. Believers who value souls do tithe. The 10 percent was created to put meat or food in God's house so that God's house has power to fulfill the great commission, "Go into all the world and preach the good news so that all might be saved" (Mark 16:15).

> **Alpha Males are needed to reverse the curse and restore the power to God's house.**

By not tithing, members are disabling their church from accomplishing its calling. For example, my chair was designed to hold my weight by using all four legs. If my church is only seeing

20 percent or less tithing families, it is similar to me trying to sit on a chair with only one leg. I would be focused on balancing instead of winning. Born again believers declare that they have the spirit of Christ living in them. If this is true, then they cannot help but to tithe and be generous on top of that. John 3:16 says for God so loved the world that he gave...... not 10 percent but 100 percent.

If 100 percent of born again **believers** designated the first 10 percent of their income, we would live in a different world. The best part of it would be that the world would recognize that it was God's people that changed the evil to good. This is a game changer and needs the influence of Alpha Males to accomplish.

Real Influence

In my humble opinion, both the world and the Church have defined influence incorrectly. We both recognize Sunday morning attendance as a mile marker of influence for a church, like it is a great thing to be able to fill a nice air-conditioned, video and audio enhanced, child friendly, glazed and jelly filled donut, coffee-laden building with people. It is like going to the movies and not having to buy a ticket and getting free drinks, popcorn, and a show! You also get the added benefit of seeing your friends as you view the show each week. Oh yes, a religious check mark is a nice thing to receive before you leave as it soothes your conscience from the week's activities spent in the world's system.

May I make a suggestion? What if we measured **real influence** as the ability to lead people where they do not necessarily want to go, but where they really need to go for the good of their family as well as society? Could it be that the definition of real influence is not leading people to a free experience that costs them absolutely nothing, but rather to a decision that will cost them a huge sacrifice in order to fulfill God's great commission?

George Barna research indicates that only 4 percent of all people that consider themselves born again believers actually give 10 percent or more to the preaching of the gospel. This means that 90 percent of most congregations actually benefit from the other 10 percent of

> **Maturity does not come with age; it comes with the acceptance of responsibility.**

their congregation's sacrifice. Think about it. The chairs we sit on, the air conditioning we use, the nursery our children enjoy, the carpet and tile we walk on, the videos, the preaching, the coffee, the bulletins, the leaders/staff, the landscaping, the entire building we can come to each week, all free of charge, comes from the 10 percenters.

How does this make you feel reading this? Well if you are a 10 percenter you probably wish the others would get on board so we could do more for the Lord. If you're a 90 percenter, you are probably wishing this chapter was not directed at you.

Manhood and Christlikeness are synonymous because Christ took responsibility for my sins not His. When will the people that enjoy the sacrifice of Christ begin to sacrifice for Him and take responsibility for a lost and dying world?

Barna also tells us that only 2 percent of all "born again believers," have ever shared their testimony much less vocally witnessed for Christ in an attempt to help others become "born again." If these numbers are accurate, and I believe they are, then this equates to 95 percent of our congregations on Sunday mornings never sharing their faith!

So I ask you, what are we actually doing on Sunday mornings in America? Is this really **influential**? We have more churches in America today than ever before and yet the crime rates are higher than ever before. The officials in office are seemingly more corrupt and passing corrupt legislation, most recently in the areas of pro-choice abortion mandates and same sex marriages. Who elected them? Americans. Who attends our churches? Americans.

To assume that a church with 2,000 attendees on Sunday mornings with 10 percent committed members is more influential than a church with 300 attendees that has 100 percent committed members is an obvious mistake. However, society and the Church buy into this deception as they both promote the pulpit that is largest, based on a Sunday morning service attendance number.

Did Jesus have a Sunday morning crowd? Did He rather go to the hi-ways and hedges? The first churches were small groups held in homes. The Book of Acts said that the believers brought their land and earnings to the home groups and shared all things with everyone in need for the sake of furthering the Gospel. How did we get off track? What have we, the American church, become? We were initially placed on the earth to be a thermostat not a thermometer. We are here to change the world not become like them. The lines are now gray instead of black and white. Our influence has become small.

Today is the day we begin to draw the lines again as we did in the beginning when Joshua stated, "As for me and my house, we will serve the Lord" (Joshua 24:15). Come on Alpha Males!

Solutions

It seems to me that for way too long the American church has wandered into the land of the unbalanced. What I mean is the Church and its leaders have **overcommitted to the uncommitted**. We have done this with resources, time, talent, and treasure. Sure we need to reach the lost, the uncommitted, with everything we have like God did when He invested His best by sending His Son Jesus as a ransom. However, once someone has declared for Christ, the fruit should be that they are willing to sacrifice for the cause of Christ. You have heard that the road to heaven is narrow and the road to destruction is broad. Instead of cultivating a culture for the broad seats (no pun intended) we should be pouring into the committed, the sacrificial, the narrow path people so that we can reach more with much better efficiency and effectiveness.

Gideon had to have his numbers decreased. So did David and Abraham. The trimming down of the core has been and still is a way in which to prepare for a real victory. Look at the Green Berets, the Delta Force, Navy Seals, and the Army Rangers. These are all small factions but the best trained of our military numbers.

The Chinese church has exploded and yet they are not allowed to preach under the penalty of imprisonment. It is called the "underground church." This church is comprised of thousands of small home gatherings of disciples that really embrace the Book of Acts style of church as well as, for the most part, the same sacrificial spirit that makes the church "The Church."

Let the Revolution begin! Being a male is a matter of birth. Being a Man of God is a matter of Choice!

1. *Will you be mentored/trained? Recruit and train others?*
2. *Will you live your convictions?*
3. *Will you commit until the job is finished?*
4. *Will you speak up and out?*

These are questions that need to be acted on and championed by Alpha Males. These are the real questions of our generation that need to be answered by heroes, people who act in a moment of time on a need greater than themselves. We are not only speaking of social injustices here that deal with race or sex, we are dealing with the highest priority in life: **eternity**.

CONCLUSION

GET READY FOR WAR

"You have not lived until you have done something for someone who can never repay you." - John Bunyan (1628-1688), English Puritan

"I was once young and now I am old, but not once have I been witness to God's failure to supply my need when first I had given for the furtherance of His work. He has never failed in His promise, so I cannot fail in my service to Him." - William Carey (1761-1834), Baptist Missionary to India

"You can give without loving, but you cannot love without giving." -Amy Carmichael (1867-1951), Irish missionary

"We make a living by what we get; we make a life by what we give." - Winston Churchill (1874-1965)

"No person was ever honored for what he received. Honor has been the reward for what he gave."

- Calvin Coolidge (1872-1933), 30ᵗʰ President of the United States

"Generosity during life is a very different thing form generosity in the hour of death; one proceeds from genuine liberality and benevolence, the other from pride or fear." - Horace Mann (1796-1859), American educator and politician

"Our culture values the size of the gift, but God values the size of what we keep." - Ed Owens, Chicago Fund manager

"I believe it is every man's religious duty to get all he can honestly and to give all he can." - John D. Rockefeller, Sr. (1839-1937)

"Giving is more than a responsibility – it is a privilege; more than an act of obedience – it is evidence of our faith." - William Arthur Ward (1921-1994)

"When I die, if I leave behind me ten pounds…you and all mankind [may] bear witness against me, that I have lived and did a thief and a robber." - John Wesley (1703-1791), English Evangelist and Founder of Methodism

Say to the nations far and wide:
"Get ready for war!

Call out your best warriors.
Let all your fighting men advance for the attack.
¹⁰Hammer your plowshares into swords
and your pruning hooks into spears.
Train even your weaklings to be warriors.
¹¹Come quickly, all you nations everywhere.
Gather together in the valley."
And now, O LORD, call out your warriors!
(Joel 3:9-11)

I leave you with this thought, *If not you then who? If not here then where? If not now, then when?*
The best time to plant a tree was actually ten years ago. The second best time is today.

Carpe Deim: Seize the Day

Psalm 90:12 says, "So teach us to number our days, that we may apply our hearts unto wisdom."

James 4:14 says, "Whereas ye know not what *shall be* on the morrow. For what *is* your life? It is even a vapor that appeareth for a little time, and then vanisheth away" (KJV).

There are 365 days in a year of a person's life with an extra day added to each leap year. The average life span of a man today in America is seventy-eight years. This equates to 28,487 days in an average man's life.

If I am fifty years old, this means today with leap years counted, I realize that by the world's averages, I am 18,340 days old! I also realize that I am looking at around 10,130 days to remain here on earth. To accomplish my purpose in the Kingdom of God, I do not have time to waste, one second being nonproductive, being upset, in fear, offended, contentious, sidetracked from my mission…it's called the great co-mission!

The Bank

Imagine there is a **bank that credits your account each morning with $86,400.** It carries over no balance from day to day. Every evening deletes whatever part of the balance you failed to use during the day. What would you do? **Draw out every cent of course!**

Each of us has such a bank: it's called time. Every morning it credits you with 86,400 seconds. Every night it writes off as lost whatever of this you have failed to invest to good purpose. It carries over no balance. It allows no overdraft. Each day it opens a new account for you. Each night it burns

> The clock is running. Make the most of today. Let's get our lives in order so our time multiplies.

the remains of the day. If you fail to use the day's deposits, the loss is yours! We must live in the present on today's deposits. Invest it so as to get from it the utmost in health, happiness, and success.

Thoughts for success:
- *How am I physically?*
- *Purpose for being physically healthy and in good shape? (Longer I live the longer I can further God's purpose for my life).*
- *Plans to improve? Goals. First step.*

Use this same process with finances, relationships, dreams, ministry, and family.

Yesterday is history;
tomorrow is a mystery;
today is a gift that's why it's called the present!

We are eternal beings. Our most enjoyable, satisfied moment will come when we know we are in the will of God, pursuing his presence and **building His kingdom**!

Learn how to increase the value of each of your days. Teach yourself to enjoy and appreciate each day while simultaneously planning and working towards improving tomorrow's adventures.

Jesus laid down the pattern. His first thirty years were preparation for the final three, the most important. He spent thirty years getting into position to bless us. **"So teach us to number our days, that we may apply our hearts unto wisdom"** (Psalm 90:12 KJV).

THE REST OF MY LIFE WILL BE THE BEST OF MY LIFE.
I AM AN ALPHA MALE.
I WILL MAKE AN IMPACT WHILE I'M DOWN ON THE GROUND AND
STILL AROUND!

So what do you do now?

Great question! You should understand that every man is unique in his makeup and calling. This book contains truths and guidelines that act as antibiotics and stop the infection of being non-male from spreading. Since, I sincerely believe in what I'm doing, I'm going to step up and challenge you here.

<u>Your next step</u> is to avail yourself to being evaluated. That's right, tell your story. Be transparent and vulnerable and then become equipped to finally win!

I am committed to helping men win, so contact me today by email and let's set a time when we can visit: *yes personally*. BAM! Ball is now in your court. How free do you really want to be?

Your Alpha male marriage, family, and destiny are now simply waiting on you.

Adam, where are you?

To begin the adventure, write to this email: gfw@teampow-erhouse.org

POSTSCRIPT

Finally, I would be remiss if I neglected to give you one very important fact about The Ultimate Alpha Male. His name is Jesus Christ. He is the most consistent and faithful of all men. He is extremely focused and He does reach his goal. You are His goal. He was given an assignment by His Father, and he honored His Father by accomplishing it. His actions on earth could be qualified as ruthless when it comes to reaching His Father's desire, "That all men be saved."

Read this scripture in Mark and listen for the distinct Alpha male overtones:

Mark 16:15 (KJV), "And he said unto them, Go ye into all the world, and preach the gospel to every creature. He that believeth and is baptized shall be saved; but he that believeth not shall be damned."

Do you see the simplicity and the no-nonsense, direct way He speaks so that everyone can understand and make his decision? I can see John Wayne or Coach Vince Lombardi saying this in their own words!

So what is the Good News that we are commanded to preach or proclaim to every creature? Well, it's found in Romans 10:9-13.

> *That if you confess with your mouth the Lord Jesus and believe in your heart that God has raised Him from the dead, you will be saved. For with the heart one believes unto righteousness, and with the mouth confession is made unto salvation. For the Scripture says, "Whoever believes on Him will not be put to shame." For there is no distinction between Jew and Greek, for the same Lord over all is rich to all who call upon Him. For "whoever calls on the name of the Lord shall be saved."*

Jesus is simply delivering the message His father commanded Him to. He said what He would do and then He kept His word (Integrity) all the way to the cross. He acted in a moment on a need greater than self (Hero.) He sacrificed his life by the way of the painful cross, so that you and I could decide to join Him in a painless eternity called Heaven.

So what do you do now? Get on your knees and ask God the Father in Jesus' name to forgive you of all the sins you've committed against Him and people. This is called repentance. Ask Jesus to dwell in your heart as Savior as well as Lord. Commit to doing what you know as well as reading His will/Word daily and praying for direction from that Word. Your job is now to go into all the world and preach the good news to lost people who are headed straight to hell and may not even know it.

Search out a church that is led by the Spirit of God as well as a pastor that values discipleship to men. Follow him and support your team/church so that you will touch more people together.

This is what Alpha males do well. This is what I did over thirty years ago. The drive I have inside of me I attribute to being given an eternal task by God. What about you? What's driving you? Now, know this promise: "Therefore, if anyone *is* in Christ, *he is* a new creation; old things have passed away; behold, all things have become new" (2 Corinthians 5:17).

If you prayed that prayer, you are a new man. You have been given the Spirit of the Ultimate Alpha Male, Jesus Christ. There is nothing you cannot do. You have a new mandate: get up and tell others the Good News of Jesus Christ!

ABOUT G.F. WATKINS

G.F. Watkins founded PowerHouse Church (power-housechurch.tv) as a spiritual son of the late Dr. Edwin Louis Cole, who was founder of Christian Men's Network. G.F. is also the founder of GenesisTeam.org, a ministry to help pastors and leaders succeed.

G.F. and Rose Watkins have traveled worldwide effectively ministering to men and teaching leadership principles. The Watkins have planted PowerHouse Namibia (powerhousenamibia.com) and PowerHouse Peru (powerhouseperu.org) with spiritual sons.

They have also stretched their faith to build Jordan Ranch (jordanranch.org), a $10 million dollar Christian Retreat Center.

The website for the ranch and its foundation is www.jordanranch.org. It's been called the finest Christian retreat in Texas.

G.F. has authored four books and his latest is titled "Take Your Place." He has also founded Most Dangerous Games (dangerousgames.org) and Intense Men (intensemen.com), a men's event where over 1,000 fathers and sons come together to camp, compete and be strengthened with wisdom to overcome life's challenges. This event has been taking place for the past six years during the month of March at Jordan Ranch in Schulenburg, Texas. For more information: www.intensemen.com   It is a one of a kind event and you need to see it for yourself.

Our latest ministry is HCC, or Helping Coaches Coach, in which we minister to the Texas High School Coaches in an attempt to reach the student athlete and change the culture of the campus. We partner with the FCA and financial partners. (See more at hccoach.org).

To order books or schedule G.F. Watkins, contact the church office 281-391-0095 or powerhousechurch.tv and inquire about speaking engagements. He has taught all over America, Africa, Scotland, South America, Mexico, England, Ireland, France, Hawaii, and Australia. G.F. bases out of Texas.

CPSIA information can be obtained at www.ICGtesting.com
Printed in the USA
LVOW04s1218030615

440889LV00002B/2/P